Wordpress and Flash 10x Cookbook

Over 50 simple and incredibly effective recipes to take control of dynamic Flash content in Wordpress

Peter Spannagle

Sarah Soward

BIRMINGHAM - MUMBAI

Wordpress and Flash 10x Cookbook

First published: April 2010

Production Reference: 1140410

Published by Packt Publishing Ltd.
32 Lincoln Road
Olton
Birmingham, B27 6PA, UK.

ISBN 978-1-847198-82-2

www.packtpub.com

Cover Image by Vinayak Chittar (vinayak.chittar@gmail.com)

Credits

Authors

Peter Spannagle

Sarah Soward

Reviewers

Ali Raza

Patrick Rushton

Sonia Munoz

Acquisition Editor

Usha Iyer

Development Editor

Chaitanya Apte

Technical Editor

Ajay Shanker

Indexer

Monica Ajmera Mehta

Editorial Team Leader

Akshara Aware

Project Team Leader

Lata Basantani

Project Coordinator

Srimoyee Ghoshal

Proofreader

Joel T. Johnson

Production Coordinator

Adline Swetha Jesuthas

Cover Work

Adline Swetha Jesuthas

About the Authors

Peter Spannagle is a WordPress consultant, technology trainer, and Web 2.0 designer. His skills include client-side coding, graphic and web design, and SEO. He also offers online marketing, training, and support services. With twelve years experience as a technology contractor, he will help you meet your goals and strives to exceed your expectations.

His professional experience includes working as the Manager of Marketing and Online Services for Youth Service California and as a Quality Rater for Google. He was also fortunate to work as part of the fabrication team for Sky Mirror (a thirty-ton stainless steel sculpture) designed by Anish Kapoor and built by Performance Structures, which debuted at the Rockefeller Center in 2006.

YourCustomBlog.com (YCB) began in 2007 to provide quality WordPress consulting services in the San Francisco Bay Area. Over the past three years, YCB has grown to servicing clients around the country and around the world.

YCB contract clients include: Singularity Hub, Sharam, The Hidden World of Girls (for the Kitchen Sisters, a segment on NPR Morning Edition), Street Soldiers Radio (on 106 KMEL San Francisco), Ustream.TV, Innovation Center Denmark (Silicon Valley), San Francisco Dream Wedding Giveaway, Legal Services for Children, The Children and Nature Network and the San Francisco Day School.

Visit my website: http://yourcustomblog.com or contact me at: info@yourcustomblog.com

I would like to thank:
My co-author, Sarah Soward
My clients, for the opportunity to assist them
My family and friends
My mentors at UC Santa Cruz and UC Berkeley
The Bay Area Video Coalition
The Flow Yoga Teacher Training program and participants
D.K. Chakravarty, Ayurvedic chef
Numi Tea and Mama Buzz
The Bolivarian Republic of Venezuela

Sarah Soward develops curriculum for and teaches the Adobe Creative Suite and design theory at the Bay Area Video Coalition (http://www.bavc.org). She has over five years experience as a technology trainer and is Adobe Certified. She specializes in creating web and print collateral for small businesses and non-profits. She is the Art Director for The Pagan Alliance, a non-profit organization, and a working fine artist (oil painting and drawing). In addition to teaching Flash, she is also an expert in the use of Dreamweaver, Fireworks, Photoshop, Illustrator, and InDesign. You can reach her at sarahsoward.com and rhinotopia.com

My Flash experience and teaching experience have come from a variety of sources. I certainly could not have done any of this without Adobe and their wonderful resources for ActionScript and Flash CS4. On that note, thanks also to Abigail Rudner. She demystified ActionScript 2.0 for me when I was first learning Flash and made my SWF's functional as well as fun.

Rose Adare gets a huge thank you for putting me on this path with the Bay Area Video Coalition (BAVC) and technology training in general. She taught me how to teach. That skill is one of the most valuable pieces of my life.

Thank you to BAVC for believing in me and keeping me and my quirky handouts around all these years.

Of course, my profs @ The California College of the Arts get props.

My Mom. I know it isn't a complete sentence. It says all it needs to say: My Mom. It's like stop(); can be this.stop(); but may not need all the extra characters to be just perfect even if it is more thorough.

Happy expressions of gratitude go out to Chris O'Sullivan, Michele Jones, their living room floor, and gluten-free donuts. Kristie Bulleit Niemeier and her dissertation progress postings get a nod as well.

Thanks to every client who ever insisted that I make something cool for them.

Finally, thanks to the man who shared this project with me: Peter Spannagle. He makes a mean cup of tea.

About the Reviewers

Ali Raza is a fresh and invigorated aspirant in the field of design, development, and authoring. He became part of the IT field at quite an early age and worked up from designing business cards, flyers, books, websites, digital maps, software interfaces, and almost all design-related things to audio and video editing, animation, and even minor 3D modeling in Autodesk Maya. Later, playing with code became his passion that compelled him to work in various programming languages including C++, Java SE, ActionScript 3, and PHP.

Ali is pursuing a Master of Science degree in Computers. He is also an Adobe Certified Instructor, Adobe Certified Expert, and Sun Certified Java Programmer.

He is currently a senior developer at 5amily Ltd., a London-based forthcoming genealogy-related social networking-rich Internet application. Previously, he has worked with different national and international advertising, telecommunication, and IT firms.

Ali is authoring an Adobe Flex 3 with AIR exam guide from the platform of ExamAids. He is also a regular author in Flash & Flex Developer's Magazine, writes project-based articles predominantly on Data Visualization, and also loves writing book reviews.

In his spare time, you will either find him engulfed in design and development-related books, or find him envisaging about the accomplishment of series of certifications in ACE Flash and ACE Dreamweaver after his masters.

I would like to express my gratitude to Packt Publishing and the authors for bringing such a wonderful title. I would also like to thank to Reshma Sundaresan, Srimoyee Ghoshal, and Chaitanya for giving me the opportunity to review this unique book. You can contact me at manofspirit@gmail.com.

Sonia Munoz is a web programmer in Valencia, Spain. She has completed her upper-Computer Systems Management and is now studying the upper development of computer applications where she is learning the Java programming language. She has worked with tools such as PHP, MySQL, HTML, CSS, jQuery, JavaScript, CodeIgniter, Joomla, Photoshop, and Dreamweaver, but is willing to learn new programming languages.

After completing her studies, she would like to start their own web development business.

Besides this book, she revised Joomla! with Flash.

For Manu, Martha, and my parents.

Patrick Rushton is a user-experience designer living in Amsterdam. He works as an Interaction Director at communications agency Dynamic Zone where he uses Flash to create brand-building online experiences that combine interactivity, motion graphics, gaming, and 3D. He blogs about web design, music, 3D modeling, and interactive television on his website, `http://www.patrickrushton.com`.

Table of Contents

Preface   1

Chapter 1: Leveraging Flash in WordPress   7
Developing a strategy to use Flash & WordPress   8
Embedding Flash .swf files in WordPress   12
Adding Flash detection with SWFObject 2.x   16
Adding Flash detection with Flash-generated JavaScript   23

Chapter 2: WordPress: Configuration and Core Plugins   27
Introduction   28
Inputting content in the Visual Editor   28
Extending the Visual Editor with plugins   31
Inputting content via the HTML Editor   35
Editing theme template files in the Theme Editor   36
Configuring WP for maximum SEO   38
Using the Google XML Sitemaps plugin   41
Using the SEO Title Tags plug-in (Version 2.3.3)   42
Using the Breadcrumb NavXT plugin (Version 3.2.1)   44
Use Google Analytics in WordPress   46
Backing up your site   48

Chapter 3: Image Galleries and Slideshows—Using Plugins and Flash   51
Introduction   52
Importing your photos from Flickr: Simple Flickr plugin (Version 1.1)   53
Using lightbox effects: WordPress Multibox plugin (Version 1.3.8)   57
Creating effects in Flash   60
Using Flash to create watermarks   66
Image thumbnails, galleries, and watermarking: NextGen gallery
plugin (Version 1.3.5)   70
Building an image gallery in Flash in the timeline   73
Building an image gallery in Flash with XML   77

Adding slideshows: Featured Content Gallery plugin (Version 3.2.0)   81
Building a basic slideshow in Flash in the timeline   86
Building a slideshow in Flash with XML   89

Chapter 4: Video Blogging + Flash Video Encoding, Skinning, and Components   **97**
Introduction   98
FLV Embed (Version 1.2.1)   98
WebTV plugin (Version 0.6)   103
Free WP Tube (Version 1.0)   105
Encoding with the Adobe Media Encoder   107
Using preset skins   113
Using Video Component buttons to customize your skin   122

Chapter 5: Working with Audio—Using Plugins and Flash   **129**
Introduction   129
WPAudio Player plugin (Version 1.5.2)   130
µAudio plugin (Version 0.6.2)   132
PodPress plugin (Version 8.8.1)   134
Using buttons in the Common Library   137
Adding sound effects to a button   140
Adding sound effects to the timeline   142
Streaming sound and coding a simple On/Off music button   144
Designing your own stylish MP3 player   146
Coding your own stylish MP3 player   151

Chapter 6: Flash Applications   **157**
Introduction   157
WP-Cumulus (Version 1.22)   158
Tagnetic Poetry plugin (Version 1.0)   161
Flexi Quote Rotator plugin (Version 0.1.3)   163
Creating a custom Quote Rotator using XML   167
WP sIFR (Version 0.6.8.1)   172
XML Google Maps plugin (Version 1.12.1)   176
Integrating Google Maps into your Flash document   179
Datafeedr Random Ads V2 (Version 2.0)   184
WP Flash Feed Scroll Reader (Version 1.1.0)   186

Chapter 7: Flash Themes   **189**
Introduction   189
CSS   190
Template files and theme structure   194
Template tags   196

Customizing Kubrik   198

Chapter 8: Flash Animations   209
Introduction   209
Creating a shape tween   210
Creating a classic tween   211
Creating a motion tween   214
Using the Motion Editor   216
Using motion presets   218
Animating with the Bone tool   219
Animating inside movie clips   221
Creating a button   224

Appendix A: WordPress Resources   227

Appendix B: Flash Resources   231

Appendix C: Shortcut Keys   233
WordPress Visual Editor keyboard shortcuts   233
WordPress HTML Editor keyboard shortcuts   234
WordPress Comment Moderation keyboard shortcuts   235
Flash keyboard shortcuts   235
Windows keyboard shortcuts   237
Mac keyboard shortcuts   237
Firefox keyboard shortcuts   237

Appendix D: Site Planning   239
Goals   239
SEO Planning   240
Functional Requirements   240
Aesthetic Requirements   240
Site Outline   241

Index   243

Preface

This book helps you create a contemporary, functional, and memorable site. Detailed instructions are provided for each section. We show the big picture by providing context, best practices, and strategies.

Learn how to work with XHTML in WordPress, configure WordPress for maximum SEO, edit theme template files, and back up your site. Our crash course in theme customization provides you with an introduction to CSS, WordPress theme hierarchy, and template tags.

More than 7,000 plugins currently exist for WordPress. We provide you with a shortlist of essential tools for creating a dynamic and media-rich website or blog, and show you how to implement these tools on your site.

The sections on Flash are intended to give you the option to create custom `.swf` files, giving you an alternative to plugins that already exist.

What this book covers

Chapter 1 helps you develop a strategy to use Flash in your WordPress blog. Learn how to embed a `.swf` manually or by using a plugin.

Chapter 2 demonstrates how to set up and work with WordPress, including creating posts and pages, and editing `.php` theme templates. We offer strategies for configuring WordPress and ways to extend the admin tools via plugins. By the end of the chapter, the user will be able to effectively use WordPress as a Content Management System (CMS) and in conjunction with Flash.

Chapter 3 shows you ways to share individual images and collections of images as thumbnails, galleries, and slideshows—using WordPress or working in Flash.

Chapter 4 shows you how to use video plugins, including video players, embed `.flv` and `.swf` files, and video blogging. Encoding through the use of the Flash Media Encoder for reduced file sizes and creation of `.flv` files is covered along with using Flash's default skinning options and editable video components.

Chapter 5 shows you how to work with audio in WordPress and in Flash. Topics covered include using a Flash audio player and creating a podcast as well as how to design your own unique audio player in Flash.

Chapter 6 explores a broad range of applications including unique ways to display your tags, how to use fonts outside of the limited set of web-only fonts, quote rotators, ad management, scrolling RSS feed displays, and more.

Chapter 7 presents an in-depth look at each of the three elements that WordPress themes are made up of: CSS stylesheets, template files, and template tags. We then apply this knowledge by customizing the default Kubrik theme.

Chapter 8 covers creating your own Flash animations for your blog. The focus here is on animating in the Flash timeline and helping you with the fundamentals of Flash animation.

Appendix A covers WordPress resources.

Appendix B covers Flash resources.

Appendix C covers shortcut keys.

Appendix D gives you a few tips on site planning.

What you need for this book

You will need a working installation of WordPress 2.8.6 or later and Flash.

Who is this book for

This book is for WordPress users interested in learning how to create a unique and media-rich site using plugins and Flash. Strategies and techniques presented are appropriate for both personal and business blogs. The intended audience has intermediate technology skills, such as a working knowledge of XHTML, CSS, and graphic design. Some familiarity with WordPress is required, as we do not address the basic mechanics of using WordPress. Previous experience with Flash is helpful but not required.

The book is written with the following users in mind:

▶ New or experienced bloggers: Get started with WordPress then take your site to the next level with plugins, theme customization, and animations.

▶ Individuals and small businesses: We help you use WordPress for more than blogging as a Search Engine Optimized and a fully customizable CMS.

▶ Site administrators: People responsible for managing content in WordPress for a company or organization will find useful tips to distinguish and add finesse to your site.

- ▸ Website developers: People who are new to WordPress or designers who want to create innovative WordPress sites for their clients.

- ▸ Multimedia blogs: How to use WordPress to share multimedia content (images, audio, video, animations, video blogging, and podcasting).

- ▸ Flash users: Those new to WordPress will learn about the many ways Flash and WordPress can work together.

Conventions

In this book, you will find a number of styles of text that distinguish between different kinds of information. Here are some examples of these styles and an explanation of their meaning.

Code words in text are shown as follows: "We can include other contexts through the use of the `include` directive."

A block of code will be set as follows:

```
function goForward(event:MouseEvent):void{

if (slides_mc.currentFrame == slides_mc.totalFrames) {

slides_mc.gotoAndStop(1);

} else {

slides_mc.nextFrame();

}

}
```

New terms and important words are introduced in a bold-type font. Words that you see on the screen, in menus, or dialog boxes for example, appear in our text like this: "clicking the Next button moves you to the next screen".

Warnings or important notes appear in a box like this.

Tips and tricks appear like this.

Reader Feedback

Feedback from our readers is always welcome. Let us know what you think about this book, what you liked or may have disliked. Reader feedback is important for us to develop titles that you really get the most out of.

To send us general feedback, simply drop an e-mail to feedback@packtpub.com, making sure to mention the book title in the subject of your message.

If there is a book that you need and would like to see us publish, please send us a note in the SUGGEST A TITLE form on www.packtpub.com or e-mail suggest@packtpub.com.

If there is a topic that you have expertise in and you are interested in either writing or contributing to a book, see our author guide on www.packtpub.com/authors.

Customer Support

Now that you are the proud owner of a Packt book, we have a number of things to help you to get the most from your purchase.

Downloading the Example Code for the Book

Visit http://www.packtpub.com/files/code/8822_Code.zip to directly download the example code.

 The downloadable files contain instructions on how to use them.

Errata

Although we have taken every care to ensure the accuracy of our contents, mistakes do happen. If you find a mistake in one of our books—maybe a mistake in text or code—we would be grateful if you would report this to us. By doing this, you can save other readers from frustration, and help to improve subsequent versions of this book. If you find any errata, report them by visiting http://www.packtpub.com/support, selecting your book, clicking on the let us know link, and entering the details of your errata. Once your errata are verified, your submission will be accepted and the errata added to the list of existing errata. The existing errata can be viewed by selecting your title from http://www.packtpub.com/support.

Piracy

Piracy of copyright material on the Internet is an ongoing problem across all media. At Packt, we take the protection of our copyright and licenses very seriously. If you come across any illegal copies of our works in any form on the Internet, please provide the location address or website name immediately so we can pursue a remedy.

Please contact us at `copyright@packtpub.com` with a link to the suspected pirated material.

We appreciate your help in protecting our authors and our ability to bring you valuable content.

Questions

You can contact us at `questions@packtpub.com` if you are having a problem with some aspect of the book, and we will do our best to address it.

1
Leveraging Flash in WordPress

In order to set up the self-hosted version of WordPress (WP), you need a host that supports PHP (v.4.3+) and MySQL (v. 4.1.2+). If you want to set up multiple WordPress installations (or use other database-driven software), you will probably want a host that offers multiple MySQL databases.

 We suggest a Linux-based (Apache) server. Make sure you get enough storage—at least 1GB. Additional utilities that are helpful for WordPress-based sites include PHPMyAdmin (for working with your database) and SimpleScripts (for installing and updating WordPress).

In this chapter, we will cover:

- Developing a strategy with Flash and WordPress
- Embedding a `.swf:` via Kimili plugin
- Adding Flash detection with SWFObject 2.0 and embedding the `.swf`
- Adding Flash detection with Flash-generated JavaScript and embedding the `.swf`

Developing a strategy to use Flash & WordPress

Identify your user level and a specific application. Develop an SEO strategy. Determine what files need to be configured and modified to achieve your goals.

Getting ready

There are an unlimited number of ways to use WordPress and Flash together. The needs, ideas, and abilities of no two users will be the same. The limits are determined by you—by your skill level and the goals you set.

The first step is to identify your level of familiarity with the Web and Multimedia design software. Be honest in your self-assessment—and don't be discouraged, no matter where you are starting today. Understanding your user level allows you to set reasonable expectations. Take a look at the following figures to understand your user level. With practice and experience, by accessing the many free resources available online and through training tools (such as this manual), you will increase your level of proficiency.

You may be a new blogger, or may have been blogging for years. You may be an admin user supporting a team using WP for business or organizational needs, a theme designer, or a plugin developer. This book is written with you in mind, assuming that you are familiar with WP basics, or are willing to become so.

Level	Type	Skills	Application		
Basic	new blogger	Little to no experience with administering a website	Publish content		
	experienced blogger	Can effectively use a CMS to manage online content	Extend WP with plugins		
Intermediate	admin user	edit code in a text editor, use a FTP client, batch resize/rename and unzip compressed files	theme modification		
Advanced			theme design	coding CSS and XHTML	write a custom theme
			plugin design	coding CSS, XHTML and PHP	write a WP plugin

new user	Little experience with the Flash interface. Little or no coding experience.	animated banner add				
			designer	Can design, do animations, and add interactivity in the timeline. Has an understanding of action script	Create a slide show/image gallery. Work with audio & video.	
					Flash developer	Can create interactivity and animations through ActionScript. Also incorporates other coding languages/files as needed.
Basic	Intermediate				Advanced	Writing a theme or plugin

How to do it...

Flash takes care of your dynamic media needs, and WordPress makes it easy to administrate your site. The way to use them together is with SEO in mind.

In terms of density of information presented to a search engine, Flash is not as effective as XHTML, in spite of recent advances. A Flash animation can have a description tag, however, properly marked up XHTML that uses `<h1>` and `<h2>` to emphasize keywords and phrases, as well as including links to and from authoritative sources, will still have more SEO value when compared to a `.swf`.

Many industries and audiences expect or require Flash animations. Your marketing and SEO strategy should determine how you mix WordPress and Flash. The goal is content that people can read and enjoy that is also understood by engines and robots. For those of us who administer or develop websites, ease of use is also a consideration.

How it works...

In your design, when blocking in space for animations, consider how they are both dynamic and static. An animation does what it does, however lovely it is, and nothing more. Once a user has seen the animation, there is often no reason to pay attention to it again. WordPress offers dynamic content—areas of the page that highlight and excerpt the most recent content from different areas. This encourages users to revisit and explore your site for new content and to pay special attention to dynamic content areas. While an animation measures change in frames per second, WordPress allows your users to measure the changes made since their last visit. In this sense, Web 2.0 represents a true change in technology—transforming the screen itself into an animation that you program—simply by publishing new content.

So, some Flash is almost always fine. But too much Flash is less useful to search engines, relative to XHTML. Additionally, Flash animations generally take more time to update than regular WordPress content.

There's more...

There are other ideas about how to combine Flash and WordPress, which we will touch on in later and more advanced chapters. Our approach should be applicable to the majority of users.

Where to place the .swf?

Flash media can be included anywhere in a WordPress theme: in the header, in a post or a page, in a sidebar, or in the footer. It takes some time to become familiar with your theme files—determining which PHP templates are called when different parts of the screen are clicked. An overview of how WordPress works is useful.

A theme has at least three views, which represent the steps to a given piece of information, moving from home page to a category to a post.

A WordPress home page is traditionally a dynamic display of updates from interior sections (like a dashboard). It can also be a static page. It's often named `index.php` or `home.php`.

The category archive view is a dynamic display of the posts in a category. It sounds complicated, but it is logical. When a user clicks on a category, not one piece of information is returned, but many. This template is called `category.php`.

The archive view is so named because, though this piece of information may be featured in other parts of the site, the user has now arrived at the URL for an individual post. The URL can be used in links or bookmarks to refer back to this specific piece of information. Typically, the format is a long-reading pane.

`page.php`, `sidebar.php`, `header.php`, and `footer.php` work just like you'd think.

Edit and debug with Firebug

Knowing which PHP templates create pages on your blog is the first step to inserting a Flash animation directly into theme files. The next step is to determine specifically which `<div>` will contain the animation. Firebug helps us match up the correct `<div>` tag with the correct PHP template.

Get Firebug here: `http://getfirebug.com/`

Firebug is an add-on for Mozilla Firefox. This handy tool allows you to see the CSS and XHTML that make up any page by context-clicking (*right-click* in Windows or *Ctrl-click* for Mac) and choosing "Inspect Element." The window splits at the bottom. Bring your mouse down to the bottom-left pane. Hovering over a `<div>` tag causes the screen to be highlighted: blue for `<div>` width and height, purple for margins, and yellow for padding. Clicking on the blue `<div>` tag loads the bottom-right pane with entries from the CSS stylesheet that control its appearance. It is helpful to have such a visual representation to understand the structure of a site.

Viewing the source (PC: *Ctrl-U*/Mac: *Cmd-Opt-U*) of a WordPress blog can be a confusing experience. Keep in mind that the XHTML output is different than the component PHP. Your templates are not what you see when you "View Source"—rather, you are seeing the result of dynamic PHP calls as XHTML, styled according to CSS. This is what makes WordPress dynamic—there are no webpages. There are only PHP templates waiting to output your website, recreated each time as the most recent content.

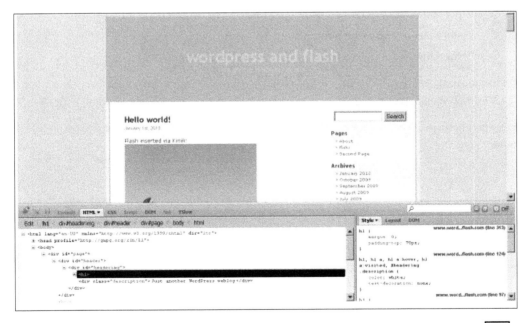

Additional utilities

There are additional utilities we will be using throughout this book; a FTP client and a text editor are required for intermediate to advanced applications. Dreamweaver is an excellent tool for coding, if you have it. A fast running stand-alone text editor specific to coding has its own merits. Here are open-source utilities for Mac and for PC:

FTP Client: FileZilla, `http://filezilla-project.org/download.php`

Text Editor: Windows comes with Notepad and Mac has TextEdit, but these text editors are not set up to code for the Web. A text editor for coding gives you access to many additional tools and options, such as line numbers, keyboard shortcuts, and auto-formatting.

- ▸ *PC*: NotePad ++, `http://notepad-plus.sourceforge.net/uk/site.htm`
- ▸ *Mac*: jEdit, `http://jedit.org`

See also

- ▸ *WordPress Theme Hierarchy*, Chapter 7

Embedding Flash .swf files in WordPress

The most basic and fundamental way of using WordPress and Flash together is to insert an animation. The steps are:

1. Create an animation in Flash.
2. Export the animation as a `.swf`.
3. Upload the `.swf` to your server.
4. Embed the `.swf` in your site.

WordPress makes it easy to embed a `.swf`—here, we provide an in-depth review of the Kimli Flash Embed Plugin, (version 2.0.2) based on Swfobject 2.x.

If you do not have an animation to begin with, this section uses a sample Flash animation, found in the `Chapter 1` folder.

Getting ready

WordPress displays Flash the same as any other web page—through Flash Detection. Flash developers use swfObject 2.x and JavaScript for Flash Detection. Otherwise, non-specialists can use one of a variety of plugins to embed Flash media (SWF or FLV). Kimli Flash Embed is among the best of such plugins.

The easiest way to embed Flash in WordPress is through the plugin "Kimili Flash Embed for Wordpress."

```
http://kimili.com/plug-ins/kml_flashembed/wp
```

"Built upon the SWFObject javascript code, it is standards compliant, search engine friendly, highly flexible and full featured, as well as easy to use." Quoted from `http://kimili.com/plug-ins/kml_flashembed/#usage` (2009).

How to do it...

Installing Kimili Flash Embed (KFE) on your WordPress site is simple.

1. In your dashboard sidebar, use the downward pointing arrow to expand **Plugins** and then click on **Add New**.

2. In the **Search** bar, type: **flash**, as seen in the following screenshot.

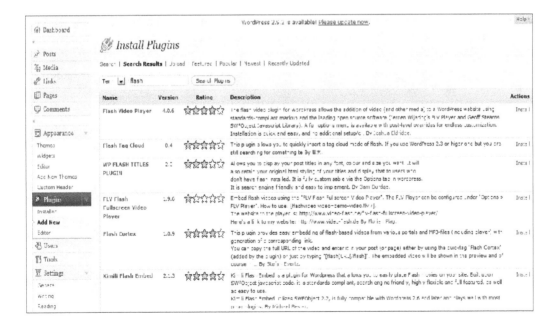

3. Browse down to **Kimli Flash Embed**, click **Install**, and then **Activate**.

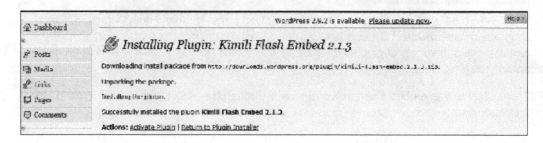

4. Now that the plugin has been uploaded and activated, the final step is to insert a Flash file in the `.swf` format.

5. Click on **Posts | Edit** and then the relevant post title (we will be using the default Hello world! post).

6. Click on **HTML** to enter the HTML view.

To add a Flash animation, use the following shortcode, replacing path, y and x parameters with the respective path, height, and width of your swf:

```
[kml_flashembed movie="/path/to/your/movie.swf"
height="y" width="x" /]
```

7. The `movie` parameter is the only one required—height and width are optional. Though it is most efficient to size your `.swf` during export, the height and width parameters will resize a `.swf` file. If you do so, be sure to keep the numbers in scale proportion to avoid distortion For reference, look at the following screenshot.

8. If you're using the Visual Editor to write your posts, look for the red Flash button on the right. Click to launch the KFE Tag Generator, a wizard-like interface that will assist you in creating the necessary KFE tag. Again, the only necessary parameter is the URL to the .swf file you want to display.

That's it! You have now inserted your first Flash animation inside WordPress. It's easy to do through the shortcode or the KFE Tag Generator. Open another tab (PC: *Ctrl + T* /Mac: *Cmd + T*) to confirm:

How it works...

Three main sections comprise the KFE Tag Generator: SWFObject Configuration, SWF Definition, and Alternative Content.

Configuration options are covered in more detail in the following section, *Adding Flash Detection with SWFObject 2.x*. Please see the *How to do it...* section.

Adding Flash detection with SWFObject 2.x

Detect which version of the Flash Player a viewer has available and supply alternative content in the event that the necessary Player is not available. The alternative content, in this case, will be a link for the viewer to acquire the appropriate Flash Player, if desired. To assist in expressInstall of the Player, the .swf will be registered with SWFObject. This method of setting up Flash Player detection does not require the use of a plugin and gives you easy and direct access to the generated code.

SWFObject 2.x is an open-source application brought to you by Google. To view the open-source license for SWFObject 2.x, please visit `http://www.opensource.org/licenses/mit-license.php`. For further information on SWFObject and for another download source for the files needed to enable it to work, please visit `http://code.google.com/p/swfobject/`.

For supplemental information regarding SWFObject 2.x from Adobe, please visit `http://www.adobe.com/devnet/flashplayer/articles/swfobject.html` for an article entitled *Detecting Flash Player versions and embedding .swf files with SWFObject 2.0*, created by Bobby Van Der Sluis.

Getting ready

In the `Chapter 1` folder, make sure that you have access to the following files: `swfobject_test.swf`, `expressInstall.swf`, `swfobject.js`, and `detection_generator.htm`. They are located inside the `Detection with SWFObject` folder.

Move the `swfobject_test.swf`, `expressInstall.swf`, and `swfobject.js` files to the root level of your theme folder. Technically, the `.swf` you are embedding can be located anywhere, as long as you use the absolute URL in your code.

The `detection_generator.htm` file holds the open-source application that generates the necessary Flash Player detection code for you to put into your PHP template.

Be aware that hand coding your live website is a great way to learn and a fast way to work. You are probably going to make a few mistakes the first time through. It is in your best interest to have all of your information backed up before editing your site. You may want to have a text editing program or a WYSIWYG editor like Dreamweaver to maintain and organize copies of your files at each stage of development.

Another option is to set up WordPress locally so that the program runs on your computer instead of a server. XAMPP is a cross-platform utility that can help set up the Apache web server on your computer. You can download it here: `http://www.apachefriends.org`.

The benefit of this approach is that you do not have to upload files via FTP or reload pages to see the changes you've made. Also, your work in progress will be private—no one will be able to see your site until you move your completed site from the local install to your server.

How to do it...

1. Open the `detection_generator.htm` file. To do this, either double click on the file or drag it onto your web browser icon:

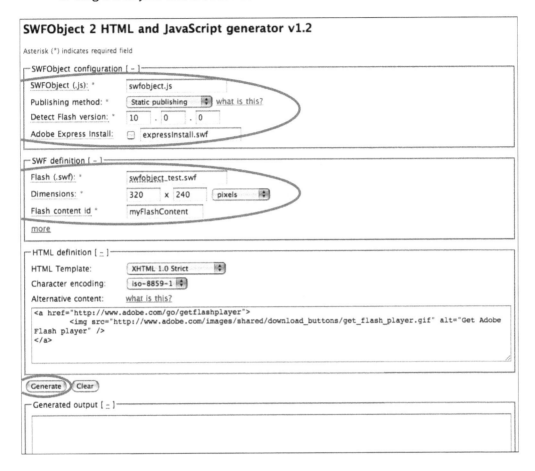

2. For the **SWFObject configuration** section, leave the default settings for **SWFObject (.js)** as **swfobject.js** and for **Publishing method** as **Static Publishing.** Change **Detect Flash Version** to the version of the Flash Player appropriate for your animation. For example, the default of 9.0.0 is adequate. If you are using the latest and greatest capabilities of Flash CS4, instead change the version to **10.0.0**. Check the box for **Adobe Express Install** and leave the file name as it is. This can be seen in the above screenshot.

3. For the **SWF definition** section, change the name of the **Flash (.swf)** to the name of your `.swf` file. In this case, change it to: `swfobject_test.swf`. **Dimensions** need to be changed to the width and height of your `.swf` file. Change this to **320 x 240** pixels. **Flash content id** can stay as the default. This can also be seen in the above screenshot.

4. For the **HTML definition** section, do not change anything.

5. Click the **Generate** button to generate the necessary Flash detection code in the window at the base of the application. Kimili generates the code and puts it into your WordPress shortcode. The SWFObject 2.x generator gives you direct access to your code. You then have to copy/paste the code to the appropriate location in your chosen template in WordPress. Your code should look like the following:

```
<!DOCTYPE html PUBLIC "-//W3C//DTD XHTML 1.0 Strict//EN" "http://
www.w3.org/TR/xhtml1/DTD/xhtml1-strict.dtd">
<html xmlns="http://www.w3.org/1999/xhtml" lang="en"
xml:lang="en">
 <head>
 <title></title>
 <meta http-equiv="Content-Type" content="text/html;
charset=iso-8859-1" />
 <script type="text/javascript" src="swfobject.js"></script>
 <script type="text/javascript">
 swfobject.registerObject("myFlashContent", "10.0.0",
"expressInstall.swf");
 </script>
 </head>
 <body>
       <div>
           <object classid="clsid:D27CDB6E-AE6D-11cf-
96B8-444553540000" width="320" height="240" id="myFlashContent">
               <param name="movie" value="swfobject_test.swf" />
               <!--[if !IE]>-->
               <object type="application/x-shockwave-flash"
data="swfobject_test.swf" width="320" height="240">
               <!--<![endif]-->
                   <a href="http://www.adobe.com/go/getflashplayer">
                       <img src="http://www.adobe.com/images/shared/
download_buttons/get_flash_player.gif" alt="Get Adobe Flash
player" />
                   </a>
               <!--[if !IE]>-->
               </object>
               <!--<![endif]-->
           </object>
       </div>
   </body>
</html>
```

6. Select the <div> tag in the body section of the code. Everything from <div> to </div> gets selected. Copy this (Edit | Copy or *Ctrl-C*).

7. In the sidebar of your WordPress Dashboard, click on the arrow to the right of Appearance. Then, click on Editor.

8. On the right side of the screen, you now have a list of all the templates that are in the root directory of the Theme folder. Click on the title of the desired .php file. This loads it in the **Theme Editor**.

9. Paste the code you copied from the code generator (Edit | Paste or *Ctrl-V*) into the appropriate Template and <div> tag. Refer back to *Developing a Strategy: Where to Place a .swf?* if needed.

10. For the head content, select and copy the following:

```
<script type="text/javascript" src="swfobject.js"></script>
 <script type="text/javascript">
 swfobject.registerObject("myFlashContent", "10.0.0",
"expressInstall.swf");
 </script>
```

Back in WordPress, open up header.php by clicking on **Appearance | Editor | header. php**. Paste the selected text in the head section after the </style> tag and before the </head> tag.

How it works...

The code generator creates the code for you based on the choices you make. It generates the code within the basic structure of an HTML page. The code generated is web standards compliant and supports the incorporation of alternative content.

The JavaScript elements in the <head> section of the .htm generated HTML output accesses the swfobject.js file. This is a library of JavaScript necessary for the Flash Player version detection process to take place. The JavaScript elements also register your .swf file with the library and tell it which version of the Flash Player is needed.

In the body section of the document, a <div> tag is created that holds the object and nested object information/method that delineates which .swf is to be played, the width and height of it, and what alternative content to display if the appropriate Flash player version is not found. Notice that special coding is used to account for the needs of Internet Explorer, for example: <!-- [if !IE] >-->

There's more...

Using relative vs. absolute dimensions

If you want have your .swf dimensions relative (in percentages) instead of absolute (in pixels), you have two choices:

Choice #1:

1. Go back into the `detection_generator.htm` file.

2. Change the **Dimensions** to **100 x 100 percentage**, as seen below.

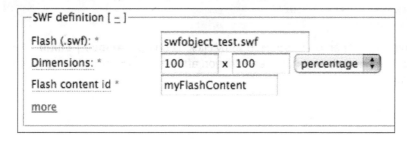

3. Click **Generate**.

4. Copy/paste your new code as needed.

Choice #2:

In WordPress, change the dimensions in pixels to dimensions in percentages. That section of code should look like this:

```
<object classid="clsid:D27CDB6E-AE6D-11cf-96B8-444553540000"
width="100%" height="100%" id="myFlashContent">
            <param name="movie" value="swfobject_test.swf" />
            <!--[if !IE]>-->
            <object type="application/x-shockwave-flash"
data="swfobject_test.swf" width="100%" height="100%">
            <!--<![endif]-->
```

Dynamic Publishing instead of Static Publishing

The default setting for the `detection_generator.htm` file is for Static Publishing. The other choice is Dynamic Publishing. Static Publishing is able to reach a larger audience because of the way it is constructed. There is less dependency on JavaScript. The downside is minimal. As per Adobe's Bobby Van Der Sluis, Static Publishing does not have a solution for click-to-activate mechanisms. However, those are already being phased out of use (Internet Explorer and Opera were the browsers of interest with this). Dynamic Publishing relies more heavily on JavaScript, even for embedding the .swf file, so the audience reached is smaller. A couple of perks are that it generates less code and has no issue with click-to-activate mechanisms.

1. All you have to do to change the publishing method is open the `detection_generator.htm` file and change **Publishing method** to **Dynamic Publishing**, as seen below, leave the defaults as desired, and click **Generate**.

```
SWFObject configuration [ _ ]

SWFObject (.js): *          swfobject.js
Publishing method: *        Dynamic publishing ⬍  what is this?
Detect Flash version: *     10      . 0      . 0
Adobe Express Install:      ☑  expressInstall.swf
HTML container id: *        myAlternativeContent      what is this?
```

2. Notice there is slightly different and slightly less code:

```
<!DOCTYPE html PUBLIC "-//W3C//DTD XHTML 1.0 Strict//EN" "http://
www.w3.org/TR/xhtml1/DTD/xhtml1-strict.dtd">
<html xmlns="http://www.w3.org/1999/xhtml" lang="en"
xml:lang="en">
    <head>
        <title></title>
        <meta http-equiv="Content-Type" content="text/html;
charset=iso-8859-1" />
        <script type="text/javascript" src="swfobject.js"></script>
        <script type="text/javascript">
            var flashvars = {};
            var params = {};
            var attributes = {};
            swfobject.embedSWF("swfobject_test.swf",
"myAlternativeContent", "320", "240", "10.0.0", "expressInstall.
swf", flashvars, params, attributes);
        </script>
    </head>
    <body>
        <div id="myAlternativeContent">
            <a href="http://www.adobe.com/go/getflashplayer">
```

```
          <img src="http://www.adobe.com/images/shared/download_
buttons/get_flash_player.gif" alt="Get Adobe Flash player" />
          </a>
        </div>
      </body>
    </html>
```

3. Copy/paste the necessary parts of this code into WordPress.

    ❑   For the head section, copy/paste everything from
        `<script type...` to `</script>`

    ❑   For the body section, copy/paste everything from
        `<div...` to `</div>`

Hitting the "More" Button

More options are available to you in the **SWF definition** section of the code generator. Click the **More** button to see them (they will look like the image below):

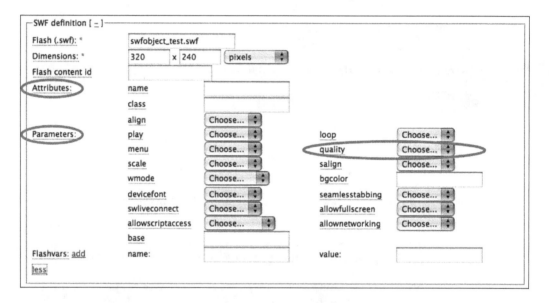

Choose and change **Attributes** and **Parameters** here if you would like the generator to create even more code for you. Many of these options are most useful when the `.swf` you are embedding is going to be the sole content of the `.html` page.

If you are doing a test run, you may want to change the **quality** setting to **low** to cut down on load time. Just remember to turn it back to the default or **high** when you are ready for the real deal.

See also

▶ *Using the Kimili plugin to incorporate a .swf*

▶ *Adding Flash detection with Flash-generated JavaScript*

Adding Flash detection with Flash-generated JavaScript

If you want to add Flash player detection to your web page, but do not want to reference an external file, this recipe offers an easy solution. Use the Flash Professional IDE to generate the `.html` page for you that contains JavaScript to detect a Flash player and will play your `.swf`. Then, copy/paste the needed code into your template in WordPress.

Getting ready

Make sure you have access to the `javascript_test.fla` file so that you can open the file and allow Flash to generate additional files in that same location. It is currently located in the `Detection with Flash JavaScript` folder inside the folder for `Chapter 1`. Change the location of this file as you need.

How to do it...

1. In Flash, go to **File | Open**. Navigate to the `javascript_test.fla` file (or use your own `.fla` file) and open it.

2. Go to **File | Publish Settings**.

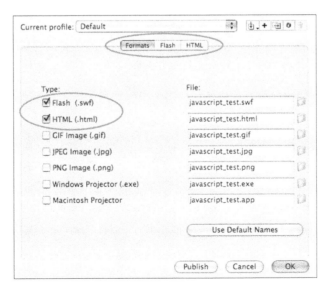

3. Make sure that **Flash** and **HTML** are checked, as shown in the previous screenshot.

4. Click on the **Flash** tab at the top of the dialog box, as seen below.

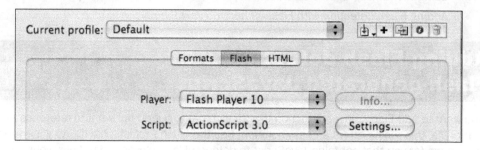

5. In the top section of the dialog box now showing, set the **Player** to the version you are targeting.

 In order for Flash to generate the appropriate code, you must target Flash Player 4 or higher.

6. Click on the **HTML** tab at the top of the dialog box, as seen below.

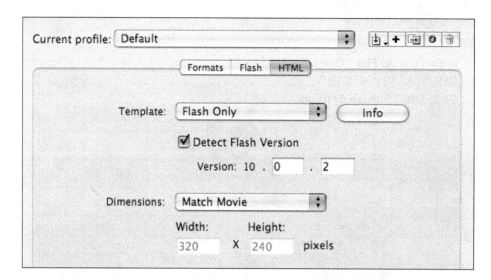

7. In the top section of the dialog box now showing, set the **Template** to either **Flash Only** or **Flash HTTPS**, check the box for **Detect Flash Version**, and type in the specific version of Flash to be targeted.

8. Click **Publish** at the bottom of the dialog box. A `.swf` file and `.html` file have now been created for you. The `.html` file holds a reference to the `.swf` as well as the JavaScript necessary for basic Flash Player detection.

9. The `.swf` can be moved to the root level of your site as needed.

10. Copy/paste the Flash detection code into a Template in WordPress.

   ❑ For the head section, copy/paste everything from `<script>` to `</script>`

   ❑ For the body section, copy/paste everything from `<script>` to `</noscript>`

How it works...

You enter the necessary preferences for your .swf and .html files into the Publish Settings dialog box. When you click **Publish**, Flash generates the requested files. As long as the `.html` template you publish is either **Flash Only** or **Flash HTTPS**, the `.html` file will be generated with JavaScript, set up to detect the Flash Player you specified. If the appropriate Flash Player version is not detected, alternative information is displayed so that the viewer has the option to download the targeted and necessary version of the Flash player.

See also

▶ *Using the Kimili plugin to incorporate a .swf*

▶ *Adding Flash Detection with swfObject 2.x*

2
WordPress: Configuration and Core Plugins

This chapter demonstrates how to set up and work with WordPress, including creating posts and pages and the basic editing of `.php` theme template fles. It offers strategies for configuring WordPress and ways to extend the admin tools via plugins. By the end, the user will be able to effectively use WordPress as a CMS (content management system) and in conjunction with Flash.

In this chapter, we cover WP configuration and settings:

- ▶ Inputting content in the Visual Editor
- ▶ Extending the Visual Editor with plugins
- ▶ Inputting content in the HTML editor
- ▶ Editing template files in the Theme editor
- ▶ Configuring WP for maximum SEO
- ▶ Using the XML sitemap SEO plugin
- ▶ Using the custom titles, SEO plugin
- ▶ Using Google Analytics in WordPress
- ▶ Using the breadcrumb navigation SEO plugin
- ▶ Backing up your site

Introduction

In Chapter 1, we outlined a strategy for using WordPress based on the relative strengths and weaknesses of WP and Flash. Boiling down the advantages of WP, we find that it's easy to update and (when used strategically) can help you get indexed in the major search engines for your targeted keywords and phrases. Flash is limitless with regards to design (though it takes time to become proficient with animation software), but a Flash site is not as well understood by robots and search engines. We introduced the use of two "views" in the WP dashboard—**Visual Editor** or **HTML**. Now, we look under the hood for more detail. It is not our intention to provide here a comprehensive guide to using WP, but instead to share some of our favorite tips and tricks for setting up WP as a CMS and for working with Flash. Also, we want to demonstrate ways of working with your site—both the content (posts and pages) and theme files. We review a number of plugins that extend the WordPress core to help you work smarter. We'll also show you how to create and implement a SEO strategy in WP to complement your use of Flash in WP.

Inputting content in the Visual Editor

Getting ready

In case you aren't clear on the difference yet, here is a screenshot showing how to navigate between the **Visual** or **HTML** editor for posts and pages:

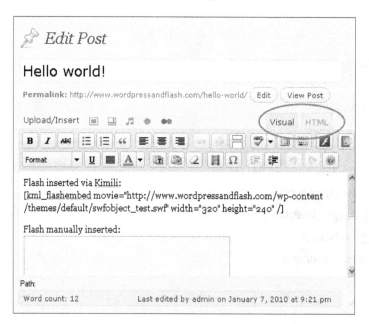

If you intend to work primarily in the WordPress Visual Editor, there are a few points to keep in mind.

WP can create XHTML on the fly, making it nearly as easy to update a web page as it is to type an email. Making website administration available to people who don't know XHTML is a great leap forward for usability on the Web.

Unfortunately, such auto-generated code can have many undesired formatting issues. Ultimately, there is no substitute for a basic understanding of the structure and syntax of XHTML.

Even if you plan on primarily using the Visual Editor, there may be times when it is necessary to take a look at the raw code. One of the most common errors is the accidental inclusion of unnecessary styles. If the Visual Editor is acting strangely, checking the code for extraneous tags is the first place to start. See *Learning XHTML,* at the end of this section, for helpful resources.

How to do it...

Type text directly into WordPress for consistency. It is often preferable to use the *Full Screen mode* (a square screen icon to the right of the spell check button; PC: *Alt-Shift-G*). If you copy and paste text from a word processor or browser into WP, you may be surprised to see that you get more than just the text. The font styles (font family, colors, spacing, and so on) and URLs are included. This may seem convenient, but often ends up creating more trouble than it is worth, since it can lead to stylistic inconsistencies.

Copy and paste into HTML view or into a text editor to remove all formatting. Then, re-style as appropriate.

After entering your text, insert images. Next, apply styles in this order: URLs, bold, unordered list (bullets), blockquote, indent, heading 2 or heading 3. This will help you to avoid the unintended application of styles.

Open up the Kitchen Sink (PC: *Alt-Shift-G*) to access additional Visual Editor tools. One important Visual Editor tool is the pull-down menu that allows you to easily apply headings. Look for the left-most button in the second row that appears when the Kitchen Sink button is clicked. Following is a screenshot highlighting the Full Screen Mode and the Kitchen Sink buttons.

How it works...

When you input and style content using the Visual Editor, you are not seeing the whole picture. Keep in mind that additional styles may be applied to your content based on one or more CSS stylesheets. Inline styles are formatting that get applied before (instead of) the rules from the CSS stylesheet. When you copy text from a word processor or browser, the content gets inline styles that will be prioritized. This can create chaos. A site looks best when it has unity of design—dissimilar fonts or colors can distract your users and detract from your message.

Most of your styling should be taken care of by CSS. A CSS stylesheet is a library of the special formatting styles used in your theme. CSS style sheets control the formatting of your content, and allow for site-wide changes by modifying this library of styles. CSS is most effectively applied externally—separate from your XHTML. External styles are referenced in between the <head> and </head> tags (normally, in a file called header.php) in the following manner:

```
<link rel="style sheet" type="text/css" href="example.css" />
```

The best strategy and technique is to use the Visual Editor in conjunction with your CSS stylesheet, and to mark up content for SEO purposes—to highlight what your content is about. This means using bold, links, and the h2 and h3 tags to denote emphasis.

Extending the Visual Editor with plugins

Depending on your operating system and browser, there is a chance that you or a client may not be able to use the WordPress Visual Editor. In other cases, you may want more control over the tools to format web content. In either case, it is possible to extend or replace the WP WYSIWYG with third-party plugins to achieve your goals.

Getting ready

The Visual Editor can be replaced or extended via plugins to give you more control. There were problems with earlier versions of the Visual Editor in the older versions of Safari that might also require the use of a third-party plugin.

> *In early versions of Safari, the visual rich editor would cause the browser to crash immediately upon loading the Write interface. This was due to a bug in Safari, not WordPress. Since the WordPress developers had no way of correcting this, they chose to disable the visual rich editor for Safari users.*
>
> *From:* `http://codex.wordpress.org/FAQ_Troubleshooting`

Use Safari 3.0.4+ with WordPress 2.3+ to avoid this problem. Or, use the free open-source browser FireFox (available here: `http://www.getfirefox.com/`). Alternatively, use the plugin *Dean's FCKEditor For Wordpress* to replace the WP Visual Editor.

```
http://wordpress.org/extend/plug-ins/deans-fckeditor-for-wordpress-
plug-in/
```

TinyMCE Advanced is another plugin that extends the Visual Editor, adding additional formatting options and allowing you to rearrange the buttons in the order you prefer. TinyMCE Advanced preserves additional buttons (such as the Kimili Flash Embed) added to the WP Visual Editor, while FCKEditor has its own built-in Flash uploader. If you're using the FCKEditor, you do not need the Kimili plugin.

How to do it...

How to use Dean's FCKEditor (version 2.5.0)

1. Click on **Plugins | Add New** and search for "FCKEditor".
2. Click **Install** and **Activate**.
3. Configuration can be found in the dashboard sidebar, under **Settings | FCKEditor.**

If you are most often linking to content that is off-site, one suggestion is to set the **Default link Target** to **New Window (_blank)**.

This ensures that visitors do not leave your site when visiting another URL, but instead open another window, as demonstrated below:

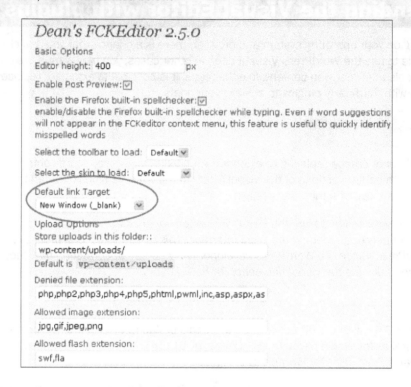

Some of the most useful tools available include:

Special Characters, Horizontal Lines, Anchors, Forms, Templates, and Replace.

Another reason to use the FKCEditor is that it allows you to paste from Word—with auto-detection cleanup.

To switch between HTML view or the FCKEditor Visual Editor, click the **Source** button, as seen in the following image.

To upload Flash using the FCKEditor, simply click the Flash logo. If this is difficult to identify, hover over the buttons for tooltips—look for **Insert/Edit Flash**.

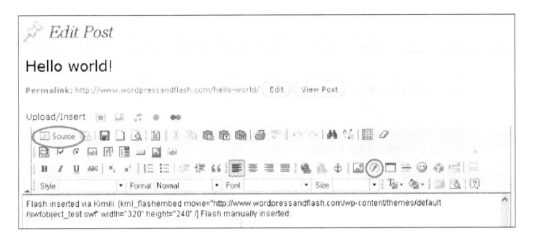

Here, we insert our sample Flash animation via Dean's FCKEditor:

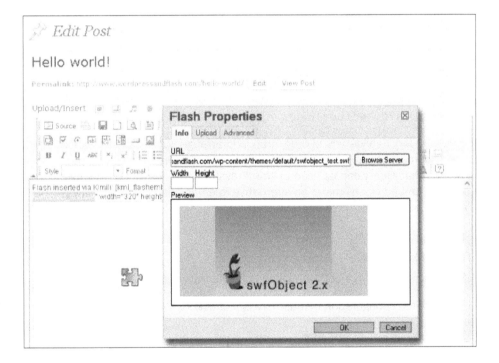

A handy chart explaining all the buttons on the toolbar can be found here:
`http://docs.fckeditor.net/FCKeditor_2.x/Users_Guide/Quick_Reference`

How to use TinyMCE Advanced (version 3.2.4)

1. Click on **Plugins | Add New** and search for "TinyMCE."
2. Click **Install** and **Activate**.
3. Configuration can be found in the dashboard sidebar, under
   Settings | TinyMCE Advanced.

TincyMCE adds fifteen plugins to the WP Visual Editor. The most useful of these include: Advanced Image, Advanced Link, Context Menu, Layers, and Paste from Word. The TinyMCE Advanced homepage is: `http://www.laptoptips.ca/projects/tinymce-advanced/`

How it works...

Dean's FCKEditor is based on the FCKEditor, a fast and lightweight open-source application for creating XHTML 1.0. Dean's FCKEditor is multi-browser compatible, including: IE 5.5+, Safari 3.0, and Firefox 1.0+.

Visit the FCKEditor homepage at: `http://www.fckeditor.net/`

Extensive documentation for end users and developers is available at:
`http://www.docs.fckeditor.net/`

TinyMCE uses jQuery to allow you to drag, drop, and arrange buttons on the toolbar. jQuery is a free, open-source software—a JavaScript library for creating interactive web pages. There are many ways that jQuery can be used in WordPress and with Flash. For example, a jQuery plugin exists to embed Flash—this is an alternative to embedding Flash with JavaScript. See: `http://jquery.com/` for more information.

There's more...

TinyMCE also acts as a bridge between inline and external styles.

At the bottom of the configuration menu, there is a checkbox to **Import the current theme CSS classes**.

Advanced

Import the current theme CSS classes ☐

Custom CSS styles can be added in /wp-content/plugins/tinymce-advanced/css/tadv-mce.css. They will be imported and used in TinyMCE. Only CSS classes will be used, also **div.my-class** would not work, but **.my-class** will.

Stop removing the <p> and <br /> tags when saving and show them in the HTML editor ☐

This will make it possible to use more advanced HTML without the back-end filtering affecting it much. It also preserves empty new lines in the editor by padding them with <br /> tags.

This option allows you to format your content by choosing from styles defined in your theme. Earlier in this chapter (in the *How it works* section of *Inputting content in the Visual Editor*), we pointed out that the Visual Editor doesn't really show you "what you get" because CSS rules will be applied based on where your content appears. TinyMCE solves this problem by loading the CSS rules into the WP Visual Editor, effectively creating a UI to format content using CSS. Quite an amazing plugin!

It is useful to note the difference between a CSS id and a CSS class, both of which may be found in a given stylesheet. An ID can be used once on a page; a class can be used as many times as you want.

IDs have the following syntax: `#example {propety: value;}`

An example of a CSS ID is: `#mystyle {color: "red";}`

Classes have the following syntax: `.example {propety: value;}`

An example of a CSS class is: `.myclass {color: "red";}`

Please note that importing the current theme classes does not work for themes that use `@import` to load CSS. If your theme does use `@import`, you can add styles manually to `tadv-mce.css`, which can be found inside the `tinymce-advanced` folder: `tinymce-advanced/css`.

Add the class names with empty curly braces (not including the properties) using this format: `.example-class-1{}`

To get the drop-down menu of **Styles** to appear in the Visual Editor, make sure to drag and drop the **Styles** button onto the toolbar in **Settings | TinyMCE Advanced**.

Learning XHTML

XHTML basics: `http://www.w3schools.com/xhtml/`

Inputting content via the HTML Editor

Those comfortable with XHTML will often prefer to use the HTML editor, especially when checking for errors. The HTML editor can also be a convenient way to mark up your content—consider hand coding in combination with the use of quicktags.

How to do it...

If you prefer to work with XHTML directly, WP provides a handy way of marking up code via quicktags. Quicktags are buttons in the HTML editor that provide a shortcut to hand coding XHTML. Simply highlight some text and click the appropriate quicktag button to automatically create XHTML, as seen below:

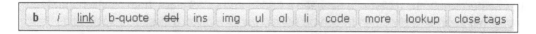

The WordPress codex covers quicktags here:
`http://codex.wordpress.org/Write_Post_SubPanel#Quicktags`

If you never want to be bothered with the Visual Editor, disable it by going to **Users** | Your Profile. The first checkbox allows you to **Disable the visual editor when writing**.

 You can use TinyMCE Advanced in conjunction with the HTML editor to gain access to both quicktags and the TinyMCE tools and customizable toolbar layout.

There's more...

It is possible to add to the default list of quicktags and even create your own keyboard shortcuts to apply your custom tags. The file that creates the default set of quicktags can be found in the `wp-includes` folder, named `quicktags.js`.

Detailed instructions on how to create custom quicktags can be found here:

`http://tamba2.org.uk/wordpress/quicktags/`

Editing theme template files in the Theme Editor

Working with content is different than editing the files that make up your theme. A theme is a "skin"—since the design is separate from the content, you can switch themes and you'll have a new look, though your content is the same (and you're still using WordPress). The structure of all WordPress themes is similar. A theme is comprised of a set of PHP files that link to CSS stylesheets and contain WordPress template tags (to insert entries from the MySQL database) and XHTML.

Like your content, these files can be modified. Additional PHP templates can be created and uploaded to your theme folder to enhance or customize your theme.

The editing of theme templates (PHP files) can be done in several ways. One way is to directly edit the files live on the server using the WordPress Theme editor. This approach is both fast and convenient, but suggested for those comfortable with hand coding. Editing template files in the Theme editor is a good way to see the immediate effects of your changes. It should be emphasized that creating backups as you customize a theme is absolutely crucial. *Backing up your site*, at the end of this chapter, reviews how to do so. XHTML is a precise and unforgiving medium—one wrong character can break your entire site.

Also, changes can be made in your favorite text editor. You can download the theme files via FTP, make your changes, and then upload via FTP. This approach is slower, but a bit safer since you can make a backup file with each change.

How to do it...

In the dashboard sidebar, navigate to **Apperance | Themes | Editor**. You will see a list of the template files on the right-hand side for the active theme, as well as a drop-down menu to select any of the other uploaded themes for editing. Clicking on a template file on the right (such as **style.css)** loads the file into the editor, as seen below:

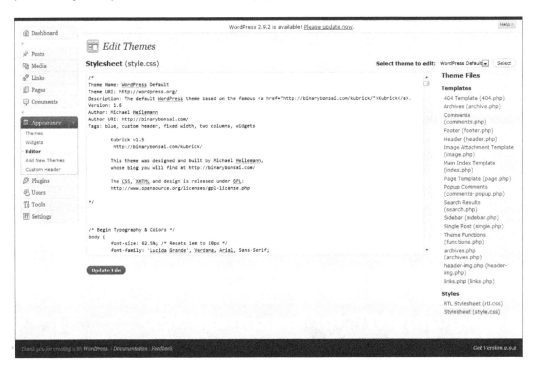

Please note that files in subdirectories are not shown. To edit files in a theme subfolder (for example, /includes), you will need to download the files via FTP, edit with a text editor, then upload the modified file via FTP.

Before making a change to any theme template, do yourself a favor and make a backup of the file you are editing. An easy way to do this is to select all (PC: *Ctrl-A*/Mac: *Cmd-A*) in the Theme editor, and paste the original code into a text editor.

Proceed with caution—and have fun!

How it works...

When you make changes to code, the best practice is to comment your code to make a record of the change. You can comment out a section of XHTML or CSS, but not PHP. Doing so means that the code will not be displayed.

A comment within a line is declared with a special `<!-- -->` tag—which in XHTML means *do not display*. Use this approach within template files to comment out XHTML.

```
<!-- Comment:  I  edited this for a reason.  Start or End  -->
```

Comments that take up multiple lines are declared with `/* */`. Use this approach in the stylesheet to comment out CSS.

```
  /* Optional: section of information.  Maybe steps, for example:
Step 1.
Step 2.
  */
```

Template hierarchy

It takes a little time to become familiar with how templates are triggered in WordPress, though the structure is meant to be logical and easy to grasp. Since your WP site serves up dynamic content, different templates are called based on the URL or where a user clicks. For example, `home.php` gets called before `index.php` on the homepage. A single post will use `single.php`, or if this is not available, `index.php`. If a user clicks on a tag, WP will look for `tag.php`, then `archive.php`, then `index.php`. This flexible structure allows you to create templates as needed.

Visit the WP codex for a complete overview of the WP template hierarchy:
`http://codex.wordpress.org/Template_Hierarchy`

Configuring WP for maximum SEO

Default WordPress settings provide a reasonable level of SEO utility. Compared to a static tables-based site or a Flash site, even the default settings are substantially more powerful. Configuring these settings maximizes the SEO potential of WP.

Getting ready

Permalinks control the URL structure of the content on your site. The default structure (`http://www.wordpressandflash.com/?p=123`) should not be used. Instead, configure shorter "pretty" permalinks that describe your content.

How to do it...

To update, configure permalinks that create user friendly SEO URLs. Take the following steps:

1. In the WP dashboard sidebar, click on **Settings | Permalinks**.
2. Click on **Day and name**.
3. Click on the **Custom Structure** field, which will now be loaded with the following:

   `/%year%/%monthnum%/%day%/%postname%/`

4. Truncate this to the following: **/%postname%/**
5. Click **Save Changes**.

For more information, visit: `http://codex.wordpress.org/Using_Permalinks`

How it works...

The preferred hosting environment for WordPress is an Apache server, such as bluehost.com. In this environment, WordPress can automatically update your `.htaccess` file.

> What is a `.htaccess` file?
>
> *.htaccess files (or "distributed configuration files") provide a way to make configuration changes on a per-directory basis.*
>
> From: `http://httpd.apache.org/docs/1.3/howto/htaccess.html`

Most simply, and in plain English, a `.htaccess` file allows you to create redirection rules for individual files or directories, including for an entire site. In a preferred hosting environment, WordPress can automatically update the `.htaccess` file. This means that each time you update your permalink structure, WordPress will make sure that the old URLs point to the new URLs.

If WP cannot automatically update your `.htaccess` file, it is most likely due to file permissions. The easiest way to update file permissions is to connect to your server via FTP and click on the file or directory for which you would like to update the permission. Right-click (PC) or Cmd-click (Mac) for the file permissions context menu. Enter or select 777 for read/write/execute.

A few notes for those of you who would like to work with the .htaccess file directly:

> ▸ Your .htaccess file must be located in your site's root directory
>
> ▸ .htaccess files must be uploaded as ASCII—not Binary
>
> ▸ .htaccess is the complete file name—depending on what text editor you are using, it may or may not support saving a file name with no extension. Don't worry—you can save as a text file and rename when you FTP.

There's more...

Configure WP to automatically ping blog search engines each time you update content. Here are the steps:

1. In the WP dashboard sidebar, click on **Settings | Writing**.
2. At the bottom of the screen, click on the link to **Update Services on the Codex**.
3. Scroll down to the **XML-RPC Ping Services** and highlight and copy the entire list.
4. Click back in your browser to return to the **Writing Settings** page.
5. In the **Update Services** field, replace the single entry (http://rpc.pingomatic.com/) with the full list.

How to create an SEO strategy

> ▸ Condense your concept to five words
>
> ▸ Do keyword research to identify allies and competitors. The Google AdWords Keyword Research Tool is a good free option: http://adwords.google.com/select/KeywordToolExternal
>
> ▸ Revise your SEO strategy: consider adding modifiers to keywords/phrases that are too competitive
>
> ▸ Example: it will be difficult to initially (or ever) rank well for a search term as broad as "organic". Adding the name of your city or neighborhood might be a good idea
>
> ▸ Metatags: keywords and description
>
> ▸ Use keywords in your page titles
>
> ▸ Mark up your content so that your keywords are in h1 and h2, in bold and as links
>
> ▸ Analyze the density of keywords on your homepage. A variety of FireFox extensions are available that do this for you. There are also websites services that will do this for free
>
> ▸ Use rel = no follow on links you prefer to not have indexed

See Also

▶ Chapter 4, *FLV Embed (Version 1.2.1)*, *How it works...* for instructions on how to set file permissions via FTP.

Using the Google XML Sitemaps plugin

We've already configured WP to automatically notify the major blog search engines each time you update or publish content. Wouldn't it be nice to do the same for the major search engines such as Google, Bing, Ask.com, and Yahoo? The same XML technology can be used to create a sitemap, or a list of pages on your site available to users and crawlers. The good news is that you can leverage a WP plugin to do so with a few clicks. The Google XML Sitemaps plugin is authored by Arne Brachhold <http://www.arnebrachhold.de/>, the homepage is: http://www.arnebrachhold.de/redir/sitemap-home/*

How to do it...

1. To add a new plugin, navigate to: **Plugins | Add New**.
2. Search for "Google XML".
3. Install and activate: **Install | Install Now | Activate Plugin**.
4. Visit the plugin configuration panel: **Settings | XML-Sitemap**.
5. Make sure to click: **Click here to build it the first time**.
6. The default settings are sufficient for most users.

How it works...

The XML sitemap is a list of all the content on your site. The name is sitemap.xml and it is located in your root directory.

An XML Sitemap is particularly important for a WordPress site, as discussed on the Wikipedia entry for site maps: http://en.wikipedia.org/wiki/Site_map

> *Some sites have a large number of dynamic pages that are only available through the use of forms and user entries. The sitemap files can then be used to indicate to a web crawler how such pages can be found.*

There's more...

Remember that WordPress is a form of dynamic publishing, using PHP. There are no static pages—instead, content is dynamically generated each time a page is loaded. The sitemap ensures that crawlers can find all of the content available on your site. All major search engines support and use the XML sitemap format. There is no guarantee that all your pages will be crawled, neither does an XML sitemap guarantee inclusion in any directory, nor a certain page rank. The sitemap is the most contemporary and effective way of communicating with search engines about the content and structure of your site. For this reason, it is highly recommended.

Using the SEO Title Tags plugin (Version 2.3.3)

The following section shows you how to use the SEO Title Tags plugin.

Getting ready

Metatags, like CSS stylesheets, are located in the head of a page—between the `<head>` and `</head>` tags. Metatags are supporting information that is not directly displayed, but describes or produces the page. Think of the head like your entry in the card catalog at the library—metatags are entries that define the language, subject, author, and so on. The title tag produces the browser title—text displayed at the top of the window, before the page content.

One important factor for on-site SEO is the `<title>` tag, a HTML tag.

The title tag has the following structure:

```
<title>Your title here</title>
```

Titles should be defined for each page on your site. The default WordPress setting is to display the post title as the title tag. This is less than ideal: your post or page titles are for humans (to describe your content), whereas the title tag is mostly used by search engines (to index a given URL). As Stephan Spencer, the author of the SEO Title Tag plugin notes on the plugin homepage `http://www.netconcepts.com/seo-title-tag-plug-in/`:

> *...post titles should be catchy, pithy, and short-and-sweet; whereas title tags should incorporate synonyms and alternate phrases to capture additional search visibility.*

The SEO title tag plugin allows you to easily define unique title tags for every post, page, category, and tag. The mass edit layout conveniently displays all the title tags in one page for instant cross referencing and comparison.

How to do it...

1. Click on **Plugins | Add New** and search for "SEO Title Tag".

2. Click **Install** and **Activate**.

3. The first step is to replace the default WordPress titles with the SEO title tag. Navigate to the Theme editor (**Appearance | Editor**) and click on **header.php**. Search for the word "title" (PC: *Ctrl-F*/Mac: *Cmd-F*). The default title will look something like this:

   ```
   <title><?php bloginfo('name'); ?></title>
   ```

4. Replace the default title tag with this call to the plugin:

   ```
   <title><?php if (function_exists('seo_title_tag')) { seo_title_
   tag(); } else { bloginfo('name'); wp_title();} ?></title>
   ```

5. Make sure to save your work by clicking **Update File**. This code ensures that the SEO title tag will be used, if available. If not, the default WP title will be used.

6. Next, visit the plugin configuration page: **Settings | SEO Title Tag.** Here, you can specify defaults for the plugin. The preconfigured settings should work for most users. If you have a lot of content, you may want to display more than 20 posts \per page.

7. Lastly, visit the Title Tag tool: **Tools | Title Tags**. This is the reason we installed this plugin—to take advantage of the super useful interface allowing you to see and modify all your titles at once. The UI is conveniently broken down by Pages, Posts, Categories, Tags, and URLs.

How it works...

The SEO title tag plugins allows you to mass edit your titles. The brilliance of this plugin is the ability to conceptualize and modify the whole set of titles at once. If you only work on one part of your SEO strategy, filling the title tags with your targeted keywords and phrases would be the area on which to focus.

The plugin adds three tables to your MySQL database:

```
wp_seo_title_tag_category, wp_seo_title_tag_tag, and wp_seo_title_
tag_url
```

Each existing WP category, tag, or URL is paired with a new field—the SEO title tag. When the page loads, the plugin checks the table for a match and outputs the SEO title tag.

Using the Breadcrumb NavXT plugin (Version 3.2.1)

Breadcrumb NavXT homepage: `http://mtekk.weblogs.us/code/breadcrumb-navxt/`

Breadcrumb navigation is a visual representation of where you are in the site. A common format is: Blog | About.

Your Categories and Pages should be highly related to your keywords. Repeating this info on each page and as a link helps to emphasize to search engines what your site is about. As we've learned, words that are links get extra SEO weight. For these reasons, breadcrumb navigation is a useful SEO strategy. Breadcrumb navigation is also useful for your human users because it helps orient them to the structure of your site and the ability to "drill down" to see content.

How to do it...

1. Click on **Plugins | Add New** and search for "Breadcrumb".
2. Click **Install** and **Activate**.

Identify the location to insert breadcrumb navigation using Firebug. Since search engines give more weight to words at the top of your page, near the top is a common approach. If you insert the code into your `header.php`, breadcrumb navigation will appear on every page.

Navigate to the Theme editor (**Appearance | Editor**) and (in most cases) click on **header.php**.

Insert the following code:

```
<div class="breadcrumb">
<?php
if(function_exists('bcn_display'))
{
    bcn_display();
}
?>
</div>
```

For our example (using the default Kubrik theme), we open `index.php` and place the breadcrumb code immediately after: `<div id="content" class="narrowcolumn" role="main">`

The end result looks like this:

How it works...

Administration takes place under **Settings | Breadcrumb NavXT**.

Here, you can control how the breadcrumb titles are formed and displayed. The format is a table, with additional tabs. First entry on the **General** tab is: **Breadcrumb Separator** – the default value is: **>**

This is a special HTML character code, producing the greater than symbol ">." A list of HTML character codes can be found here: `http://en.wikipedia.org/wiki/List_of_XML_ and_HTML_character_entity_references`

In this example, we use the alternate character code to produce the greater than symbol: **>**

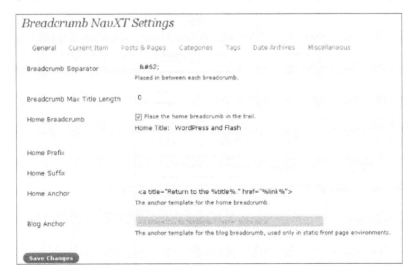

You can also set special rules for the homepage breadcrumb. The **Home Anchor** field sets the tooltip for the link to the homepage—the text that appears when a user hovers over the link. By modifying the Home title and **Home Anchor**, we get the following effect:

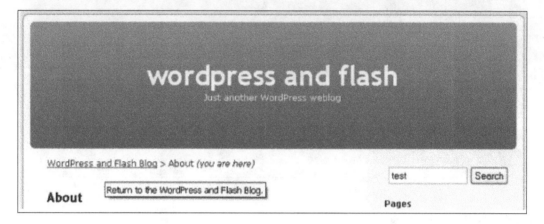

The rest of the tabs allow you to set custom behaviors for breadcrumbs. The **Current Item** tab allows you to set options for the current page. For example, you could add "(you are here)" for the **Current Item Suffix.** You can use HTML in these fields—for example, `<i>`(you are here)`</i>`.

Also, it is possible to configure special behaviors for **Posts & Pages**, **Categories**, **Tags**, and **Date Archives.**

Use Google Analytics in WordPress

Our final SEO recommendation is to use Google Analytics (GA). Though the benefit of knowing something about your visitors and how they use your site may be clear, it may not be immediately obvious how this is an SEO practice. The answer is simple: Analytics data is the feedback loop by which you fine tune or revise your SEO strategy. Once your site is designed and launched, we suggest you adjust your SEO practices based on the real-world results.

How to do it...

Google Analyticator (Version 5.1) is our recommended plugin.

1. Click on **Plugins | Add New** and search for "Analyticator".
2. Click **Install** and **Activate**.

   You will need to sign up for an Analytics account and associate a URL with it: `http://www.google.com/analytics/`

3. You do not need to copy the tracking code that is automatically generated at the completion of the sign-up and website profile creation process. Visit your Analytics homepage and copy the **UA** number (directly to the right of the website profile name of your WP site).

4. Back at your WP dashboard, click on **Settings | Google Analytics**.

5. Paste your user-specific code into the **Google Analytics UID** field.

6. In the **Google Analytics logging is:** drop-down menu, select **Enabled**. Click **Save Changes**, and you are ready to go!

How it works...

GA provides you with quite a bit of information. You select any range of days for which stats are available, and **Graph** your data by **Day**, **Week,** or **Month**. In **Table** view, you can sort your data by clicking on a column heading, as shown below.

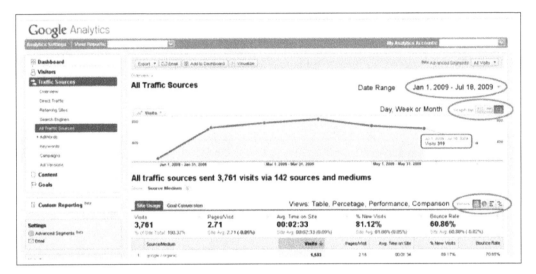

In brief, you might want to review the following areas:

Traffic Sources: How users came to visit your site (a search engine, referring site, or entering the URL directly)

Visitors | Map Overlay: A geographical representation of your user base

Content | Content By Title: Cross reference your title tags with your statistics

Backing up your site

Backing up your site is absolutely essential, especially for those for those of us who enjoy coding and customizing our site and theme. Here, we outline a strategy to back up your content in three parts: WordPress content in XML format, themes, plugins, uploads, and configuration files via FTP, and SQL backup via plugin.

Getting ready

WP-DBManager (Version 2.50) is our plugin recommendation. This excellent plugin was contributed by veteran WP plugin developer Lester "Gamerz" Chan. In addition to creating database backups, you can also optimize your database and restore an existing backup. You can even repair a database, add or drop tables, or run an SQL query from the WP dashboard.

How to do it...

To back up your content, you will need to download a file in XML format that contains your posts, pages, comments, custom fields, categories, and tags for all authors. Since your content is separate from your design, a backup in this format will allow you to import your data (only) into another WP installation, should you ever have the need.

1. In the WP dashboard sidebar, click: **Tools | Export**.
2. Then: **Download Export File**.
3. Next, a backup via FTP.
4. In the root directory, save copies of your `wp-config.php` file and the `.htaccess` file, if you have one.
5. Also, copy the entire `/wp-content` directory to back up your theme, plugins, and uploads.

Back up your MySQL database with the WP-DBManager plugin:

1. Click on **Plugins | Add New** and search for "WP-DBManager".
2. Click **Install** and **Activate**. Once the plugin is installed and activated, navigate to the **Database** menu at the bottom of the dashboard sidebar.
3. Click **Backup**. The default backup location is `wp-content/backup-db`. This can be changed from **Database | DB Options.** Here, you can also schedule automatic database backups and optimization, as well as explore more advanced interactions with your MySQL database.
4. Make sure to download a copy of your database to your computer, or have the backup emailed to you by visiting **Databse | Manage Backup DB.**

How it works...

Now, you have a copy of your theme and any modifications you've made. This allows you to utilize your design on another WP installation, or roll back your theme to a previous state. The `.htaccess` and `wp-config.php` files will allow you to recreate your site in a fresh WP install, should you ever have the need. `wp-config.php` is your admin key to WP. This file contains your MySQL database, username, and password. Keep it in a secure place. `.htaccess` is a record of all your permalink redirects—with this file, you ensure that any old bookmarks of extinct URLs will point to the updated content (WP does this automatically).

The `/wp-content` folder contains your modified theme files, plugins, and uploads.

The backup of your SQL database is like a snapshot in time—it contains everything except the WordPress software and the files you've uploaded (plugins and themes). Restoring a database will overwrite all your data, including the posts, pages, categories and comments. This is useful when moving from one server to another, in the event of hacking or other catastrophes. Restoration is a snap with the WP-DBManager plugin. Click on **Database | Manage Backup DB**, select the desired backup and click the **Restore** button.

You can also import the SQL file via PhpMyAdmin. Here is a video showing you how to do this: `http://www.dewahost.com/tutorials/cpanelx/importsqlfile.html`

3
Image Galleries and Slideshows—Using Plugins and Flash

In this chapter, we will cover the following:

- ▶ Importing your photos from Flickr: Simple Flickr plugin
- ▶ Using lightbox effects: WordPress Multibox plugin
- ▶ Creating effects in Flash
- ▶ Using Flash to create watermarks
- ▶ Using image thumbnails, galleries, and watermarking: NextGen Gallery plugin
- ▶ Building an image gallery in Flash in a timeline
- ▶ Building an image gallery in Flash with XML
- ▶ Adding slideshows: featured content gallery plugin
- ▶ Building a basic slideshow in Flash in a timeline
- ▶ Building a slideshow in Flash with XML

Introduction

Images are a major part of almost every site. In this chapter, we show you ways to share individual images and collections of images as thumbnails, galleries, and slideshows using WordPress plugins or working in Flash.

Two concepts we will be working with are DRM and XML:

- DRM stands for Digital Rights Management or Digital Restrictions Management. DRM is a strategy that limits how people can use your content. Anything you put on a public website is potentially up for grabs, so the best strategy is to share only what you want to be made publicly available. The watermarking of images, the compositing of a copyright (image or text) onto an image, is a common DRM strategy. We will show you how to watermark images using a WP (WordPress) plugin or in Flash.

  Knowing how to give proper credit for images that are not your own is also essential. The MLA standard for citing a website includes the following:

  username. imagename. Day Month Year <http://somedomain/images/image.jpg>.

- We suggest you do not use the carats when publishing online (as it conflicts with the use of the carat as a tag for XHTML). Instead, encode them correctly using special characters. See Chapter 2, *Using the Breadcrumb NavXT plugin*, the *How it works...* section.

- XML stands for Extensible Markup Language. It is closely related to XHTML, Extensible Hypertext Markup Language, which is HTML that conforms to XML standards.

- An RSS feed, which is a list of the most recent content on a website, is an example of an XML file. The list must show (at minimum) the title, URL, description, and content. If you are using "pretty" permalinks, WP sets up an RSS feed for you automatically at: `http://yourdomain.com/feed`. If you are using default permalinks, the RSS feed can be accessed at: `http://yourdomain.com/?feed=rss`.

  WordPress actually configures four types of feeds automatically. For more information, see: `http://codex.wordpress.org/WordPress_Feeds`.

- XML and XHTML work together to allow automated processes to occur. Some examples include these:
  - Notifying your RSS feed subscribers about new content
  - Importing an RSS feed of images to display on your site
  - Pulling data from a file to be animated in a `.swf`

- Using XML to populate your `.swf` makes updating images in your `.swf` very easy. Swapping images can be done painlessly and swiftly by you or by a client who has little or no knowledge of ActionScript (or even of XML). All you have to do is change the file names in the XML file. Often, this benefits you after the project is competed and makes the extra prep and knowledge required to build these Flash-XML bridges worthwhile.

A note about images for the Web: `.gif` and `.png` files are often used for transparent images or images with solid blocks of color. `.jpg` is preferable for photos.

Importing your photos from Flickr: Simple Flickr plugin (Version 1.1)

Image sharing is a key feature of many sites. Flickr is a popular and convenient tool to use to organize and share photos. The Flickr Photo Album plugin makes it easy to display your photos from Flickr on your WP blog.

Three advantages of this plugin are that you can do the following:

- Create a WP image gallery from Flickr so users will not have to leave your site to see your Flickr photos
- Insert Flickr galleries in posts or pages via handy WYSIWYG buttons
- Insert Flickr images in a sidebar

Getting ready

The plugin can be installed using the **Plugins | Add New** section of the WP admin interface and searching for "Flickr Photo Album." Alternatively, you can download the plugin from its homepage: `http://tantannoodles.com/toolkit/photo-album/`

Update your permalinks, otherwise the plugin will not work (see Chapter 2, *Configuring WP for maximum SEO*).

Make sure to have your Flickr login and password handy.

How to do it...

1. Install and activate the plugin.
2. Visit the configuration page for the plugin: **Settings | Photo Album.**
3. Click on **Flickr API key**— this will take you to your Flickr account.
4. Copy and paste the **Flickr API Key** and **Shared Secret** into the appropriate fields. Make sure you do not have any extra spaces in either field.
5. Click **Next**.
6. **Step 1:** Click on **Retrieve Flickr Permissions**.

7. You will see two messages. The correct choice reads: **If you arrived at this page because you specifically asked to connect** to your Flickr account, **click here.** Click **Next**.

8. Click **OK I'LL AUTHORIZE IT**.

9. You will see a verification message: **You have successfully authorized the application**.

10. Under **Flickr Settings**, look for **Photo Album Syndication**.

11. Under **Photo Albums**, click on **Organize Albums**.

12. Click **Yes, display my Flickr Albums on this blog**.

13. Enter the location of the post or page you have in mind. For example, you could enter flickr.

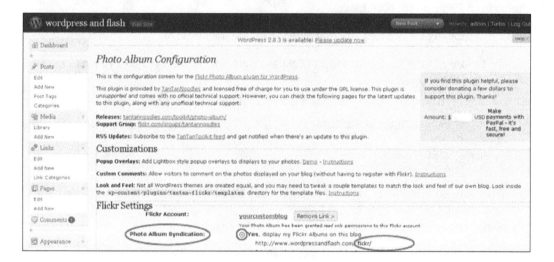

14. Click **Save Settings**.

15. This takes you to Flickr.com. Drag and drop your images to create a new album. Make sure to give your album a title and description.

16. Then, back in WordPress, click **Refresh All Albums**.

17. Click **Save Settings**.

Now, you have an image gallery from Flickr that is viewable (and cached) on your own site. The image gallery includes a slideshow feature; here is what it looks like:

There's more...

Perhaps you want to add a photo (or selection of photos) from your photostream, albums, or from another Flickr user into a WP post or page. All you have to do is click on the Flickr button in the WYSIWYG.

Adding your Flickr photos to the sidebar is a snap.

Make sure that under **Settings | Photo Album | the Flickr Settings**, **Flickr Sidebar Widget** has a check mark to **Enable the Flickr Widget for your sidebar**.

Admin your sidebar by visiting **Appearance | Widgets**.

Simply drag and drop the Flickr Sidebar widget. Click on the downward pointing arrow to the right of the widget title to expand—then, choose how many photos to display. The Sidebar should look like this:

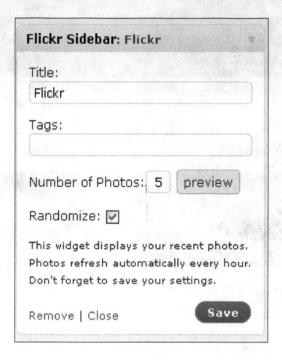

Other plugins

▶ Facebook Photos plugin: `http://tantannoodles.com/toolkit/facebook-photos/`

▶ Flickr Manager plugin: `http://tgardner.net/wordpress-flickr-manager/`

▶ Flickr Tag plugin: `http://www.webopticon.com/archives/148`

More information

To learn about working with lightbox effects, visit the advanced configuration overview located at the subversion repository for the plugin: `http://code.google.com/p/photo-album/wiki/Documentation`

Specifically, see the section labeled **Popup Overlay Support**.

Using lightbox effects: WordPress Multibox plugin (Version 1.3.8)

A lightbox is a way of displaying a gallery of images. A user clicks on a single photo, and without taking the user from the page, a full-screen gallery and slideshow takes place. A user can browse the gallery and exit the lightbox window. Our Flickr slideshow from the previous section is an example of a lightbox.

The WordPress Multibox plugin allows you to conveniently share multimedia from your WP blog with lightbox elegance and utility. It is a useful and free tool that works with the following file types:

- Images in `.jpg`, `.bmp`, `.png`, and `.gif` formats
- Flash video (`.flv`)
- Flash animations (`.swf`)
- MP3 music files (`.mp3`)
- HTML files
- PDF files
- Windows Media Video (`.wmv`)

Visit the plugin's English home page at `http://www.rutschmann.biz/php-mysql-javascript-und-ajax/wordpress-multibox-plugin-en`

Getting ready

Prepare your thumbnail and full-screen image files. The thumbnail can be up to the maximum size allowed by the container div as long as you keep in mind that CSS styles such as margin, padding, and border will constrain the total space available. Use Firefox to inspect, prepare, and revise. The full-screen version can be up to 1024 pixels—this will support most screen resolutions.

How to do it...

1. Install the plugin by visiting **Plugins | Add New**. Search for "multibox."
2. After you activate the plugin, visit its configuration page at **Settings | Multibox**.
3. Make sure to visit each of the four submenus:
   - General options
   - Design options
   - Handle PDF Files in the Multibox
   - Slideshow

4. To use the plugin, simply link to an image. As an example, we will insert an image into a post.

5. Use the Media Uploader to upload and insert the thumbnail, as is shown in this example:

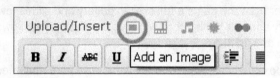

6. Set the **Link URL** field automatically by clicking on the File URL button. Then, click insert into post.

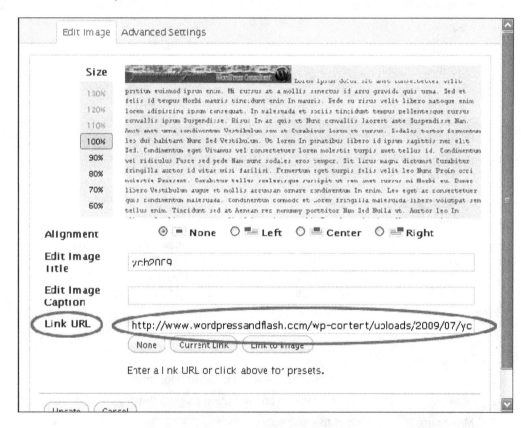

7. Next, upload the large full-screen version using the same WP media uploader.

8. If you switch to HTML view now, all you have to do is modify the `<a href>` tag (the link) to point to the large file—in our example, from `ycb2009.jpg` to `ycb2009_lg.jpg`:

```
<a href="http://www.wordpressandflash.com/wp-content/
uploads/2009/07/ycb2009_lg.jpg"><img src="http://www.
wordpressandflash.com/wp-content/uploads/2009/07/ycb2009.
jpg" alt="ycb2009" title="ycb2009" width="450" height="46"
class="alignnone size-full wp-image-31" /></a>
```

How it works...

When using the default settings, the WordPress Multibox plugin takes over the link behavior for the media file types listed above. Essentially, any image file, `.flv` or `.swf`, `.pdf`, `.htm`, `.mp3`, or `.wmv` that you wrap in an <a href> tag will be shown in the lightbox. For this reason, the Multibox plugin is not compatible with some other image plugins, such as the NextGen gallery.

There's more...

If you don't want lightbox effects for every piece of media that is a link, make the appropriate changes to the General options.

To enable lightbox effects for a specific link, simply add the mb class to the link: class="mb".

To size the lightbox window for a specific link, use the rel="" attribute, like this: rel="width:960,height:800".

A complete example using both:

```
<a class="wmp" rel="width:960,height:800" href="http://some_domain_or_
image_or_etc">This link opens in a lightbox!</a>
```

See also

▶   *Image thumbnails, galleries, and watermarking: NextGen gallery plugin*

Creating effects in Flash

It is easy to create effects such as drop shadows and bevels in Flash. These are technically referred to as filters. Filters can be applied to text, movie clips, and buttons. If you wish to apply a filter to another type of element, such as an imported bitmap image, convert it to a movie clip first.

How to do it...

1. In the Flash Professional IDE, create a new file: File | New Choose **Flash File (ActionScript 3.0)**.

2. Create an element of text, a movie clip, or a button as needed.

> To create text, use the Type Tool, set the properties (such as font size) in the Properties Panel, click once on the Stage, and type something.
>
> To create a movie clip, select any shape(s) or bitmap image(s), go to **Modify | Convert to Symbol** (*F8*), select **Movie Clip**, name the movie clip as needed, and hit **OK**.
>
> To create a button, select any shape(s) or bitmap image(s), go to **Modify | Convert to Symbol** (*F8*), select **Button**, name the button as needed, and hit **OK**.
>
> *Double click* on the button symbol instance on the Stage to isolate it and view its timeline. Edit the symbol so that it has a minimum of an **Up** state and a **Hit** state. The easiest way to accomplish this is to select the frame for the **Hit** state and insert a frame (*F5*). Here is an example of the timeline:

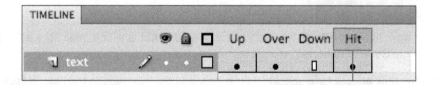

3. Make sure you select the item you are applying the filter to.

4. In the Properties panel, click on the **Filters** tab to view the **Filters** options if not already visible.

5. Click on the New Filter button at the bottom of the **Filters** section to access of the list of filters. The list of filters consists of the following:

    ❑   Drop Shadow

    ❑   Blur

    ❑   Glow

    ❑   Bevel

    ❑   Gradient Glow

    ❑   Gradient Bevel

    ❑   Adjust Color

6. Click on one of these options to apply that filter.

7. To edit the filter, adjust the value settings for the different properties listed.

8. As an example, select **Drop Shadow**. You get the following settings:

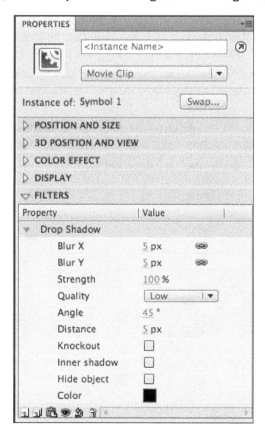

9. Adjust **Blur X** and **Y** to make the shadow more feathered/fuzzy. Higher numbers make it fuzzier.

10. Adjusting the **Strength** adjusts the opacity of the shadow. Lower percentages are more transparent. If there are other elements behind the shadow, the color of those elements will be affected by the color and opacity of the shadow.

11. **Quality** is how well the shadow is rendered. You have **Low**, **Medium**, and **High** to choose from. See what looks best and still meets your target file size and load time to maintain your frame rate in complex animations.

12. **Angle** comes in degrees and determines the location of the shadow in relation to the shape creating the shadow. You can think of it in terms of the position of the light source. The range is from zero to 360 degrees. We recommend consistency between shadowed shapes. If you use 45 degrees on one shape on your page, use 45 degrees on all the shapes on your page.

13. **Knockout** gives you a checkbox. Check the box. The shape, whether it is text, a movie clip, or a button, will be knocked out, or hidden. However, the shadow still shows up as if the shape were still present, just invisible.

14. **Inner Shadow** is a checkbox as well. Check the box, and the shadow shows up inside the shape rather than outside of it. Make sure that the shape or text to which you are applying the inner shadow is large enough for this to look reasonable.

15. **Hide Object** is another checkbox. Check the box, and the result is that the shape is hidden so that the entire shadow is shown. The shape is not knocked out, just turned invisible.

16. **Color** allows you to choose an alternate color for the shadow. Click the box of color for access to the color swatches and picker. Choose the color you desire.

17. Adjust the settings as needed, as shown below.

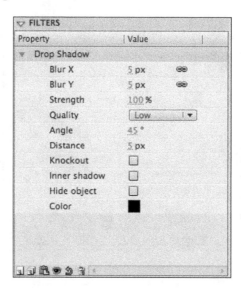

18. Save the file. Go to **File | Export | Export Movie** to create the file format you need. Testing the movie (*Ctrl/Cmd Return*) will generate a SWF.

There's more...

A single text element, movie clip, or button can have more than one filter applied to it. It is also possible to enable and disable different filters to compare and contrast the effects of each separately and together. Beyond that, if you really do not like a filter you chose, by all means delete it! Each of these tasks are completed using the buttons at the base of the Filter section in the Properties panel:

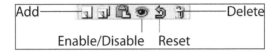

In addition to more filters, other types of visual effects can be applied manually. Also discussed below is how to add a border.

Adding, enabling/disabling, and deleting filters

More than one filter can be added to a single element.

1. Simply click on the New Filter button again, and select a different filter from the list.

 Be cautious with adding too many filters to one element. It is easy to get carried away and enter the Land of Cheese.

2. To turn off a filter, select it. Then click on the enable or disable Filter button. It looks like an eyeball at the base of the panel. It is a toggle.

3. To delete a filter, select it. Then click on the trash-can icon at the base of the panel.

4. To reset the filter settings back to their defaults, select the filter. Then click on the Reset Filter button at the base of the panel. It looks like an arrow turning back on itself.

Adding borders and exporting as a series of JPG Files

There may often be times that you want to have a border on an image. There is not a filter in Flash that makes hard borders. This must be accomplished manually. Again, this works best if all of the images are of the same dimensions. If the images differ in size, you will have more work to do, but the process is essentially the same.

While similar results can be achieved in programs such as Adobe Photoshop or similar image editing programs, this method allows you to see what each JPG will look like before you commit to it. You can know that each image will turn out well because you get to see them quickly and easily in one file before you have Flash save them separately for you. This can speed up your design process because guesswork is eliminated.

To quickly create a border on more than one image and export as JPG files, do the following:

1. Put the files you want to apply a border to into one folder.

2. Name these files sequentially (i.e.- `pic_01.jpg`, `pic_02.jpg`, `pic_03.jpg`, and so on). You are also welcome to use the demo files in the Chapter 3 images folder.

3. In Flash, create a file that has a layer reserved for images (name it `images`).

4. Select the key frame on the images layer.

5. Go to **File | Import | Import to Stage** (*Ctrl/Cmd R*).

6. Navigate to and select only the first file in the sequence. Again, feel free to use the images in the Chapter 3 images folder.

7. Hit **Import**, and you should get the following dialog box:

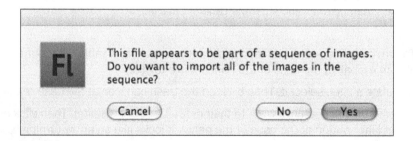

8. Select **Yes**. The images will all be placed into the selected layer, one key frame after another.

9. Select one of the images, and look at the Properties panel to get the dimensions of the selected image. It should be in the **Position and Size** option as **W:** and **H:** for width and height.

10. Create a new layer above the images layer. Name it `border`. This layer should end up having the same duration (the same number of frames) as the images layer.

11. Use the Rectangle Tool to create a rectangle with a stroke and no fill. Use the color swatches in the Tool Box to select a stroke color and no fill (the white box with the red line through it). The default stroke weight is 1px. This is the norm for border thickness. It can be edited in the Properties panel's **Fill and Stroke** section as required.

12. With the rectangle selected, set the width and height of it to match the dimensions of your images. If all of your images are the same dimensions, your work here is, basically, complete.

 If you have images of different dimensions, create key frames on the border layer that line up with images (hit *F6*). Resize the rectangles as needed.

13. Go to **Document** | **Page Properties** (*Ctrl/Cmmd J*), and make the stage match the dimensions of the contents.

14. Save the Flash file. It is always good to have a master copy.

15. Go to **File** | **Export** | **Export Movie**. It should look like the following:

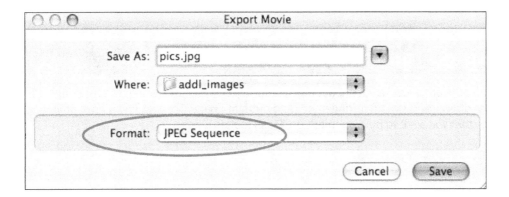

16. Choose a location to export the files to, such as a folder on your desktop.

17. For **Format**, choose **JPG Sequence**.

 If you need a different file format, this is the step in which to choose it.

18. Hit **Save**.

19. The following dialog box appears with JPG setting options:

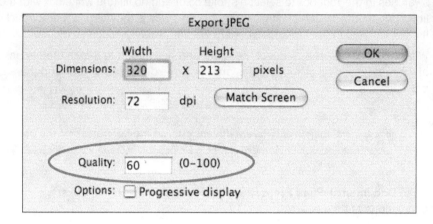

20. Choose the settings you need, such as a higher or lower setting for **Quality**. Flash will render each frame of your Flash movie into an individual JPG file.

21. Upload these images into WordPress where and how you need to.

Using Flash to create watermarks

Watermarks are a low visual impact way to inform viewers of ownership of your images. They help to dissuade copyright infringement and outright image thievery. If you have an image or a design that you want to put your mark on, Flash makes it easy.

Getting ready

Have one or more images that you want to test a watermark on available to you. A JPG file will work well. If you do not have any images, use Flash's drawing tools to create something. There are also images available to you in the Chapter 3 images folder.

How to do it...

1. Create a new file: **File | New Flash File (ActionScript 3.0)** for example.

2. Import a file: **File | Import | Import to Stage** (*Ctrl/Cmmd R*). If you get a dialog box asking if you want to import more than one image (an entire sequence of images, for example), select **No**. If you do not get the dialog box, that is fine.

3. Use **Modify | Page Properties** (*Ctrl/Cmmd J*) to adjust the stage size as desired. Check the box for **Match: Contents** if you want the stage to exactly match the size and position of the placed image file.

4. The imported image should be on **Layer 1** in the timeline. Rename that layer `image` to help keep the contents of your layer clear. To rename a layer, double click on the current name of it so that you can type.

5. Make a new layer. Name the new layer `watermark`.

6. Select the first (and, at this point, only) key frame in the watermark layer.

7. Grab the Type tool. Select the text settings you want in the Properties panel. The size of the image dictates the font size. You will be best off using font that is easy to read and consists of substantial characters. Try Arial Black over Arial, for instance.

8. Type: **copyright your name year** (for example: **© Sarah Soward 2009**).

 To insert the copyright symbol © in Flash, hold down *Alt 0169/Option G.*

9. With the text selected, open the **Filters** section of the Properties panel if it is not already open.

10. Click on the New Filter button, and select **Bevel**.

11. For Arial Black font at 20 to 36 points, try using the following Bevel Filter settings. You are welcome to experiment with other fonts, font sizes, and bevel filter settings. If more than one image is receiving a watermark, it is in your best interest to make the watermarks match:

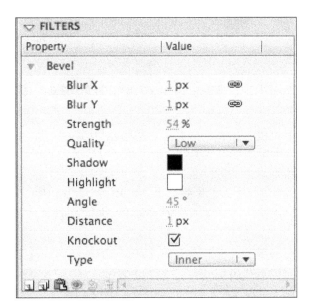

12. If you want your watermark to go diagonally across the image, grab the Free Transform Tool.

13. With the text selected, move the tool just to the outside of any corner of the resulting bounding box around the text.

14. Click and drag in the direction you wish to rotate.

15. To constrain the rotation to 45 degree increments, hold down *Shift* as you rotate.

16. Save the file. Go to **Control | Test Movie** (*Ctrl/Cmmd Return*) to create the SWF. Embed into WordPress at your leisure.

How it works...

In Flash, a layer on top of another in the timeline equates to an element visually on top of another in your document. Any image can be placed below the watermark layer to have the watermark apply to it. The watermark is mostly transparent because the **Knockout** box is checked in the **Bevel** filter. This keeps the impact of the watermark low enough that viewers are not overly distracted by it. However, it still marks the image clearly.

There's more...

It is possible to create watermarks for multiple images in Flash. This processing of multiple files is where the power of Flash is most useful. You can also export the multiple images as a sequence of JPG files. If needed, you can export as a sequence of GIF, PICT, or PNG files as well. Photographs often look best as JPG files. GIF and PNG files work great for graphic/vector work.

Watermarking multiple images and exporting as JPG Files

To quickly mark more than one image and export as JPG files, do the following:

1. Put the files needing watermarks into one folder. This works best if all of the images have the same dimensions.

2. Name these files sequentially (i.e. - `pic_01.jpg`, `pic_02.jpg`, `pic_03.jpg`, and so on). You are also welcome to use the demo files in the Chapter 3 image folder.

3. In Flash, create a file that has a layer reserved for images (name it `images`) and a layer above that with your watermark on it.

4. Select the key frame on the images layer.

5. **File | Import | Import to Stage** (*Ctrl/Cmmd R*).

6. Navigate to and select only the first file in the sequence.

7. Hit **Import**, and you should get the following dialog box:

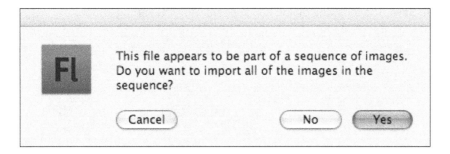

8. Select **Yes**. The images will all be placed into the selected layer, one key frame after another.

9. In the watermark layer (and any other layer you may have for design purposes), select the frame that lines up with the last key frame in the images layer.

10. Insert a frame (*F5*) so that the watermark shows up over each photo.

11. Save the Flash file. It is always good to have a master copy.

12. Go to **File | Export | Export Movie**, shown below:

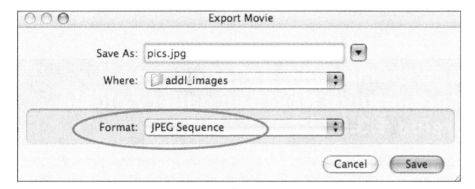

13. Choose a location to export the files to, such as a folder on your desktop.

14. For **Format**, choose **JPG Sequence**.

 If you need a different file format, this is the step in which to choose it.

15. Hit **Save**. The following dialog box appears with JPG setting options:

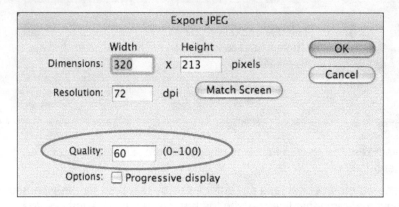

16. Flash will render each frame of your Flash movie into an individual JPG file.

17. Upload these images into WordPress where and how you need to.

See also

▸ *Image thumbnails, galleries, and watermarking: NextGen gallery plugin*

Image thumbnails, galleries, and watermarking: NextGen gallery plugin (Version 1.3.5)

The NextGen Gallery by Alex Rabe is an excellent and proven alternative to the WordPress Media Uploader. You can upload your files and automatically create thumbnails. Also, you can watermark and tag your images, share them in posts, pages, and sidebars, use a built in slideshow, and more. The plugin homepage is `http://alexrabe.boelinger. com/?page_id=80`.

How to do it...

1. **Install** and activate the plugin.

2. Visit the **Gallery** menu in your WP Dashboard sidebar.

3. You can add images by going to **Gallery | Add Gallery/Images**. There are options to manually create a gallery, upload a ZIP file of images, import a folder of images on the server, or upload files from your computer. Choose a method that works for you, and insert images into a gallery.

4. The simplest option is to enter a name for a new gallery under Add new gallery. A confirmation appears:

   Gallery portfolio successfully created. You can show this gallery with the tag [nggallery id=1].

5. Then, visit **Upload Images** to add images to your gallery.

6. In the **Upload image** field, click on **Browse**. You can repeat this step as many times as you want to add multiple images.

7. In the **in to** field, pull down to select the appropriate gallery.

8. Click **Upload Images**.

9. Visit **Gallery | Manage Gallery** to work with your new gallery.

10. You will see a list of all the existing galleries—click on the **Title** of your gallery to work with a particular one.

11. A number of useful options can be found here. For example, you can update the **Alt & Title Text / Description** for all your images at once. Another option is to bulk edit your images—place a check mark in the **ID** field for as many images as you want (or click the checkbox in the **ID** field to select/deselect all). Then, click the pull-down menu that reads **No action**. A variety of options are available, such as copy, move, resize, and delete tags. Two of the most useful are **Set watermark** and **Create new thumbnails**.

12. To configure the thumbnail options, visit **Gallery | Options | Thumbnails**

13. Watermarking options are configured by visiting **Gallery | Options | Watermark**. (watermark is a tab at the top—second from the right).

14. The menu points out that you configure in this screen, and apply in another. It also points out that this action permanently alters your images.

You can only activate the watermark under **Gallery | Manage Gallery**. This action cannot be undone.

15. You can use an image or text as a watermark, and adjust the color, opacity, and positioning.

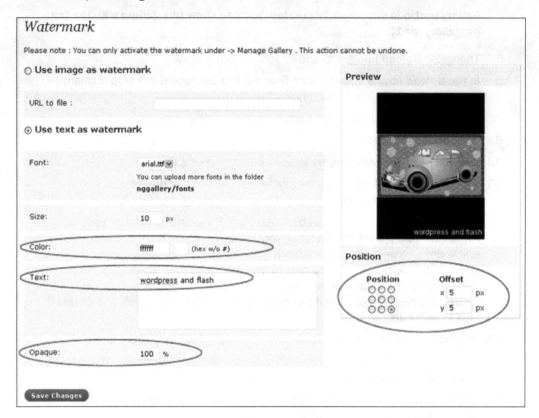

16. Check out the general options page at **Gallery | Options**.

17. You will need to configure the Slideshow settings if you see an error: **The path to imagerotator.swf is not defined, the slideshow will not work.**

18. You may need to download a script to make the slideshow work. Go here to visit the homepage of the JW Image Rotator: `http://www.longtailvideo.com/players/jw-image-rotator/`

19. Then, upload the `imagerotator.swf` to your server.

20. In the field **Path to the Imagerotator (URL)**, enter the path name. For example, `http://www.wordpressandflash.com/wp-content/uploads/`

21. You can now configure the slideshow settings such as size, duration, and transition effects.

22. If you navigate to **Appearance | Widgets**, you will see three new widgets that you can drag and drop to your sidebar: NextGen Slideshow, NextGen Widget, and NextGen Media RSS.

When you are editing a post, the insertion of an individual image, a gallery, or a selection of photos from several galleries (an album) as thumbnails or a slideshow is accomplished simply by clicking on the Add NextGen Gallery button in the WYSIWYG:

You can also use shortcode: `[slideshow id=1]`

Building an image gallery in Flash in the timeline

If ActionScript is not necessarily your strong suit, you can cut down on the amount of coding you do by utilizing the timeline in Flash's design interface. In this exercise, you will import a sequence of images and create previous and next navigation buttons.

If you would like to see a preview of the completed gallery, open `gallery_timeline.fla` in the `Chapter 3` folder.

Getting ready

Have more than one image ready to use. Ideally, the images should be named sequentially so that import is as easy as possible. Also, it is best if the images have the same dimensions so that the shift between each is not jarring. You may also use the sequential files in the Chapter 3 images folder for this lesson.

How to do it...

1. Create a new file: **File | New**. Select **Flash File (ActionScript 3.0).**

2. Rename Layer 1 as `images`.

3. Select the key frame on the images layer. Create a movie clip symbol. **Insert | New Symbol** (*Alt/Opt F8*)). Select **Movie clip**, name it `mc_slides`, and hit **OK**.

4. In the movie clip, name **Layer 1** `images` Select the first key frame: **File | Import | Import to Stage** (*Ctrl/Cmmd R*).

5. Navigate to and select only the first file in your sequence of files.

6. Hit **Import.** You should get the following dialog box. Select **Yes**. The images will all be placed into the selected layer, one key frame after another:

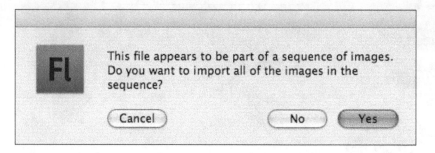

7. Click on **Scene 1** at the top left of the stage to access the main timeline.

8. Select the symbol instance of the movie clip. Name it `slides_mc` in the Properties panel. You will call this name later in the ActionScript.

9. **Modify | Page Properties** (*Ctrl/Cmmd J*) to adjust the stage size as desired. Check the box for **Match: Contents** if you want the stage to exactly match the size and position of the placed image file. Remember that buttons are going to be incorporated. If you do not want your buttons to overlap your images, make the stage large enough to accommodate your buttons. The stage can always be resized further later.

10. Position your movie clip containing the images as you like, and save the Flash file.

11. Make a new layer in the timeline. Name this `buttons`. Use the Type Tool to separately type the words `Next` and `Prev`. Position these words where you want them. These are going to become your buttons.

 Buttons can be made of almost anything. They can incorporate shapes, text, movie clips, sound, and more. In addition, you can design your image gallery to look any way you want it to look. As your own time allows and need demands, add more layers to hold background and foreground elements to dress the image gallery up a bit.

12. Select the `Prev` text. Go to **Modify | Convert to Symbol** (*F8*). For **Name**, type `b_prev` , as is shown in the following screenshot. For **Type**, select **button**, and hit **OK**:

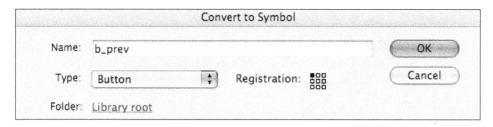

13. With the symbol selected, name it `prev_btn` in the Properties panel, like the example below:

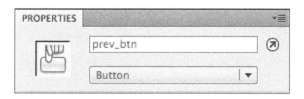

14. To edit the button so that it has a rollover state and a hit state, *double click* on it. This isolates the symbol and shows the timeline for just this one element. By default, there is an **Up** state that consists of your text.

15. Create an **Over** state by selecting the frame below the word **Over** and hitting *F6*. Change the color of the text.

16. Create an adequately sized **Hit** state by selecting the frame below the word **Hit** and pressing *F6*. Make a rectangle that is filled with color and completely overlaps the text. This provides an active area for your button that your viewer will be able to reliably hit. No one can see your **Hit** state. It does not matter what it looks like. The resulting timeline should look like the following:

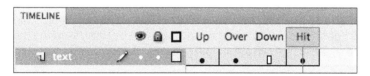

17. *Double click* on the stage to go back to Scene 1 and exit the timeline for this button.

18. Select the Next text. Go to **Modify | Convert to Symbol** (*F8*). For **Name**, type `b_next`. **Type** needs to be **button**. Click **OK**.

19. With the symbol selected, name it `next_btn` in the Properties panel.

20. Repeat steps 14 – 17 to add **Over** and **Hit** states.

Now the fun part. It is time to add ActionScript to make this thing run.

1. Make a new layer at the top of the main timeline, and name it `actions`.

2. Select the first key frame of the actions layer: **Window | Actions** (*F9/Option F9*). Type the following code into the Actions panel:

```
slides_mc.stop();

next_btn.addEventListener(MouseEvent.CLICK, goForward);
prev_btn.addEventListener(MouseEvent.CLICK, goBack);

function goForward(event:MouseEvent):void{
    if (slides_mc.currentFrame == slides_mc.totalFrames) {
        slides_mc.gotoAndStop(1);
    } else {
    slides_mc.nextFrame();
    }
}

function goBack(event:MouseEvent):):void{
    if (slides_mc.currentFrame == 1) {
        slides_mc.gotoAndStop(slides_mc.totalFrames);
    } else {
    slides_mc.prevFrame();
    }
}
```

3. Save the file. Test the movie (*Ctrl/Cmd Return*). The image gallery should go forward, backward, and loop in both directions.

The code for this image gallery allows you to add just about as many images into the timeline as you need. For the sake of load time, you probably want to keep it under hundred images. All you have to do is import additional images into additional key frames in the movie clip. Putting the images into a single movie clip symbol also makes moving and transforming all the slides at once very easy—simply move or transform `slides_mc`.

How it works...

The ActionScript in the actions layer controls the timeline. The first command the SWF is given is to stop the timeline of `slides_mc` on frame 1. From there, the rest of the ActionScript applies. When you click on a button with your mouse, the ActionScript that applies to a mouse click on that button is activated. In this case, if someone clicks on the Next button, the SWF will go to and stop on the next frame in the timeline for `slides_mc` unless it is displaying the last frame in that timeline. If it is displaying the last frame, there is not a next one, so it displays frame 1 instead, just as you told it to do when you wrote in your code. If the user clicks on the Previous button, the SWF will go to and stop on the previous frame in the timeline for `slides_mc` unless it is on the first frame. Since no frame exists before the frame 1, it loops back and displays the last frame just like you told it to do.

See also

► *Image thumbnails, galleries, and watermarking: NextGen gallery plugin*

Building an image gallery in Flash with XML

With this technical recipe, you will create an image gallery populated through the use of an XML file. This makes updating your image gallery with new images very easy for anyone, including your clients who may not have any experience with ActionScript. That said, you want to have a little experience with ActionScript for this one.

If you would like to see a preview of the completed gallery, open `gallery_xml.fla` in the `Chapter 3` folder.

Getting ready

Have images available to you and collected in one folder. JPG files will work well. Is it usually best if the images have the same dimension. There are images available to you in the Chapter 3 images folder if you prefer that. You will also need access to a text editor, such as OpenOffice, to create the XML file.

How to do it...

1. Create a folder to house your images folder that you have prepped and your soon-to-be-created `.fla`, `.swf`, and `.xml` files. Move your `images` folder into this new folder. Make sure the name of the folder is `images`.

2. In a text editor, create a new file, and save it as `gallery1.xml`. In the `.xml` file, type the following:

```
<?xml version="1.0" encoding="utf-8"?>
<slideshow>
<image picURL="images/pic01.jpg" />
<image picURL="images/pic02.jpg" />
<image picURL="images/pic03.jpg" />
<image picURL="images/pic04.jpg" />
<image picURL="images/pic05.jpg" />
</slideshow>
```

3. Make sure that you use the name of your image files if they are not named `pic01.jpg`, and so on, as in the example.

4. Save the `.xml` file to your folder that also contains your `images` folder.

5. Create a new file (**Flash File ActionScript 3.0**) in Flash.

6. **Modify | Document** to set the Stage size as needed. 380 x 300 px works well for the images in the `Chapter 3` folder. Remember to leave room for navigation buttons.

7. Name **Layer 1** `buttons`. Create two buttons: one that will show the next image and one that will show the previous image. See the Button recipe in Chapter 9 if you need instructions on how to make a button.

8. Do make sure that the previous button symbol instance is named `prev_btn` and the next button symbol instance is named `next_btn`. The names should be input into the Properties panel separately for each button.

9. Create a new layer at the top of the timeline, name it `actions`, and select the Key Frame.

10. Go to **Window | Actions** (*F9/Option F9*) to get the Actions panel. Insert the following code into the Actions panel for Frame 1 on the actions layer:

```
var total:Number;
var pics:XMLList;

var loadersArray:Array=[];
var loadCounter:Number=0;
var playCounter:Number=0;

var slideshow:Sprite = new Sprite();
var picSlides:Sprite = new Sprite();

var xml_loader:URLLoader = new URLLoader();
xml_loader.load(new URLRequest("gallery1.xml"));
xml_loader.addEventListener(Event.COMPLETE, processXML);

function processXML(event:Event):void {
    var xml:XML=new XML(event.target.data);
```

```
      pics=xml.image;
      total=pics.length();
      loadImages();
      xml_loader.removeEventListener(Event.COMPLETE, processXML);
      xml_loader=null;
   }
   function loadNext():void {
      var pic:Loader=Loader(loadersArray[playCounter]);
      picSlides.addChild(pic);
      pic.x = (stage.stageWidth - pic.width)/2;
      pic.y = (stage.stageHeight - pic.height)/2;
   }
   function startShow():void {
      addChild(slideshow);
      slideshow.addChild(picSlides);
      loadNext();
   }
   function onComplete(event:Event):void {
      loadCounter++;
      if (loadCounter==total) {
         startShow();
      }
      var loaderInfo:LoaderInfo=LoaderInfo(event.target);
      loaderInfo.removeEventListener(Event.COMPLETE, onComplete);
   }
   function loadImages():void {
      for (var i:Number = 0; i < total; i++) {
         var url:String=pics[i].@picURL;
         var loader:Loader = new Loader();
         loader.load(new URLRequest(url));
         loader.contentLoaderInfo.addEventListener(Event.COMPLETE,
onComplete);
         loadersArray.push(loader);
      }
   }
   function nextPic(event:MouseEvent):void {
      playCounter++;
      if (playCounter==total) {
         playCounter=0;
```

```
        }
        loadNext();
    }

    function prevPic(event:MouseEvent):void {
        if (playCounter==0){
            playCounter=total-1;
        } else {
            playCounter--;
        }
            loadNext();
    }

    next_btn.addEventListener(MouseEvent.CLICK, nextPic);
    prev_btn.addEventListener(MouseEvent.CLICK, prevPic);
```

11. Test the movie (*Ctrl/Cmd Return*). The gallery should be working and ready for all the pieces to go into WordPress.

How it works...

The `.xml` file populates the `.swf` file with the images listed in it. The images load directly onto the stage of the `.swf`. Positioning is controlled by the x and y coordinates. The following centers the images on the stage:

```
    pic.x = (stage.stageWidth - pic.width)/2;
    pic.y = (stage.stageHeight - pic.height)/2;
```

The next and previous buttons control which image in the list is being shown. The slideshow loops based on the conditional statements, such as the following:

```
function nextPic(event:MouseEvent):void {
    playCounter++;
    if (playCounter==total) {
        playCounter=0;
    }
    loadNext();
}

function prevPic(event:MouseEvent):void {
    if (playCounter==0){
        playCounter=total-1;
    } else {
        playCounter--;
```

```
    }
        loadNext();
    }
```

Statements that include if and else are very useful when it comes to looping. When `next_btn` is clicked, `if` the image gallery is at the last image, it will display the first image, noted as `0` in the code. Otherwise (`else`), it will display the next image listed in the `.xml` file. The same goes for `prev_btn`, except in reverse. If on image `0`, it will play the last (`total - 1`) image.

See also

▸ *Image thumbnails, galleries, and watermarking: NextGen gallery plugin*

▸ *Building an image gallery in Flash in the timeline*

▸ Chapter 9: *Buttons*

Adding slideshows: Featured Content Gallery plugin (Version 3.2.0)

We already reviewed a few ways to create slideshows of images in WP. What if you want to create a rotating gallery of your WordPress posts or pages? The Featured Content Gallery allows you to do just this—display an image, post title, and excerpt for each featured article. A single flash animation provides a navigable slideshow with links to the individual posts or pages. This is a very useful way to highlight particular or new content. Let's learn how to do it!

Getting ready

The Featured Content Gallery homepage is: `http://www.featuredcontentgallery.com/`

How to do it...

1. Search for "featured content" under **Plugins | Add New**.
2. Install and activate the plugin.

3. Use FireBug to identify where you want to insert the Featured Content Gallery (FCG). In our example, we will use `<div id="content>` (which has a maximum width of 450px) and place the FCG below `<div class="breadcrumb">`. This will cause the FCG to appear on the homepage above our posts, below the breadcrumb navigation:

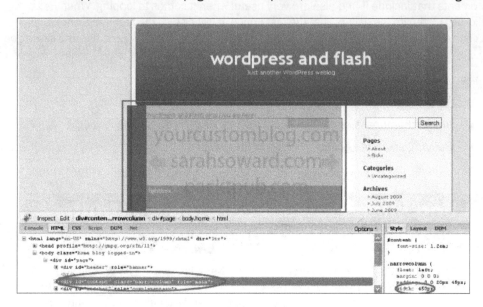

4. Navigate to **Appearance | Editor**, and insert the following code to your `index.php`, `home.php`, or as appropriate:

```
<?php include (ABSPATH . '/wp-content/plugins/featured-content-
gallery/gallery.php'); ?>
```

5. Click Update File to save your changes.

6. Next, you will have to edit each post or page you want included in the slideshow. For the FCG to work, an image must be attached to the post or page by using the custom field. Your best approach is to resize the images to be used in the FCG to fit the space. In our example, we will be using a size of 450px X 200px. You can upload the images via FTP or using the Media Uploader.

7. You must include the complete URL of the image you intend to use, and the custom field must be named **articleimg**.

8. Edit an existing post or page, and scroll down past your post or page text to the Custom Field area.

9. In the **Name** field, enter **articleimg**. After the first time, you will be able to choose **articleimg** from the drop-down menu.

10. For the value, enter the absolute URL of the image.

11. Our example is: `http://www.wordpressandflash.com/wp-content/uploads/fcg1.jpg`

12. Make sure to click Update Post to save your changes, as you can see in the following screenshot:

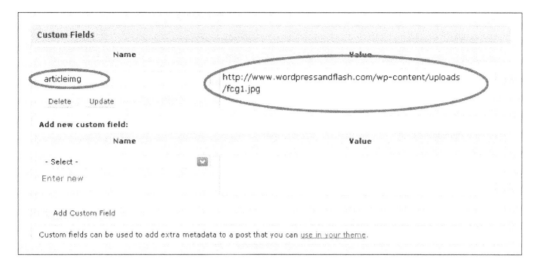

13. You must have at least two (2) items featured for the gallery to work, so repeat this step twice.

14. Now that your content is ready to work with the FCG, let's configure the plugin settings.

15. Visit **Settings | Featured Content Gallery** to configure the plugin.

16. Here, you can choose a single category to use in the FCG and set the number of items to display.

17. Alternatively, you can specify the IDs of individual posts or pages to be included, as is shown here:

Featured Content Selection - Select either a blog category or individual post/page IDs for your featured content:

◯ Select here to use category selection   ◉ Select here to use individual post or page IDs

Category Name:

Post or Page IDs (comma separated no spaces):

42,23

Number of Items to Display:

☐ Check here to randomize post/page ID display

Gallery Style - Choose your gallery size and colors:

Gallery Width in Pixels:

450

Gallery Border Color (#hex or color name):

Gallery Height in Pixels:

200

Gallery Background Color (#hex or color name):

Text Overlay Height in Pixels:

50

Gallery Text Color (#hex or color name):

Slide Transition Times and Other Options - Choose your slide and fade duration, carousel button name and text overlay

Slide Display Duration (milliseconds):

9000

(Default: 9000 milliseconds / 9 seconds)

Carousel Button Name:

WP & Flash

(Default: "Featured Content")

Slide Fade Duration (milliseconds):

500

(Default: 500 milliseconds / .5 seconds)

Number of Words in Text Overlay:

25

(Default: 100 words)

How to find IDs:

To find out the ID, edit the post or page and the URL of your browser that contains the ID. Look at the end for `"post=."` For example, the ID below is 23:

`http://www.wordpressandflash.com/wp-admin/post.`
`php?action=edit&post=23`

If you want to get the IDs for multiple posts or pages, use FireFox. Make sure you have a checkmark next to **View | Status Bar**.

Then, go to **Posts | Edit**:

Hovering over the post title brings up the URL in the Status Bar.

18. The size of the box that will display your text (title and excerpt) is controlled by the field named: **Text Overlay Height in Pixels**.

19. For instance, if we desire an overlay that is one quarter of the total height, we would use a setting of 50, since our height is 200px.

20. Click **Update Options** to save your settings.

The Multibox plugin conflicts with the FCG—you can only use one or the other.

How it works...

The FCG was created from SmoothGallery: `http://smoothgallery.jondesign.net/`.

Like the Multibox plugin, it uses the MooTools JavaScript framework.

Building a basic slideshow in Flash in the timeline

A slideshow is a series of images that appear one after another. A basic slideshow can be completed very easily in the timeline in Flash. With additional Flash design skills, you can further dress up any slideshow to enhance the visual experience of the user. Here, the focus is on providing the steps to make the slideshow functional. This recipe is for a looping slideshow. Following this recipe are additional instructions on how to stop the slideshow on the last image/frame.

If you would like a preview of a sample slideshow, open the `slideshow_timeline.fla` file in the `Chapter 3` folder.

Getting ready

Have a sequence of images available to you. JPG files will work well. This will work best if the images you use are named sequentially (i.e. - `pic_01.jpg`, `pic_02.jpg`, `pic_03.jpg`, and so on). There are images available to you in the Chapter 3 images folder if you prefer that.

How to do it...

1. Create a new file: **File | New.** Select **Flash File (ActionScript 3.0)**.
2. Rename **Layer 1** to `images`.
3. Select the key frame on the images layer.
4. Go to **File | Import | Import to Stage** (*Ctrl/Cmmd R*).
5. Navigate to and select only the first file in the sequence.

6. Hit **Import.** You should get the following dialog box. Select **Yes**. The images will all be placed into the selected layer, one key frame after another:

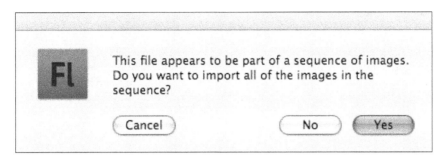

This file appears to be part of a sequence of images. Do you want to import all of the images in the sequence?

Cancel   No   Yes

7. **Modify | Page Properties** (*Ctrl/Cmmd J*) to adjust the stage size as desired. Check the box for **Match: Contents** if you want the stage to exactly match the size and position of the placed image file.

8. Save the Flash file.

9. Use **Control | Test Movie** (*Ctrl/Cmmd Return*) to generate and view the .swf. This will most likely be a slideshow that is much too fast.

10. To change the rate of the slideshow, you have a few options:

   ❑ First off, see if changing the frame rate will make it slow enough.

   ❑ Secondly, you can add more frames/more time to each of your slides.

We suggest a combo.

11. Go to **Modify | Page Properties** (*Ctrl/Cmmd J*). Change the **Frame Rate**, for instance, to 10 fps (frames per second). Hit **OK**.

12. Add 10 frames to each key frame on the images layer if you want each slide to show up for 1 second. Add 20 frames for 2 seconds, and so on.

13. To add frames, either select each key frame in turn, and hit *F5* the desired number of times, or select the key frames you want to move, and then drag them to the right in the timeline the desired amount of frames. With the second option, you will need to add more frames for the last slide by hitting *F5* either the desired number of times or on the appropriate frame. The end result in the timeline should look something like this:

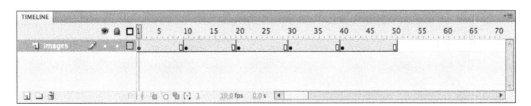

14. Continue to test the movie (*Ctrl/Cmmd Return*), and tweak the frame rate and number of frames for which the images are visible.

15. Save the Flash file.

> Images can also be converted into symbols and have filters applied to them and/or be animated as part of the slideshow presentation. You can also add a layer above the images layer to hold a watermark. For animation techniques, please see Chapter 9: *Flash Animations*.

How it works...

By default, Flash creates looping animations. All you have to do for a basic slideshow is create a sequence of images in the timeline. From there, add enough time to each image so that the viewer has enough time to see and enjoy each image. Changing the frame rate is another way to adjust how long an image is viewable. The lower the frame rate, the longer it takes an SWF to go from one frame to the next. The faster the frame rate, the more quickly the transition from one frame to the next occurs. Basically, 10 frames per second is like going 15 miles per hour. 24 frames per second is like going 60 miles per hour. You can absolutely travel the same distance and see the same things—one method simply takes less time than the other.

There's more...

If you would a slideshow that does not loop, as this one does by default, continue on to the next steps.

Stopping the loop

With any looping slideshow or animation, the following steps apply in order to stop the looping default function of a SWF:

1. Have any looping FLA file open in Flash.

2. Create a new layer at the top of the timeline. Name it `actions`.

3. In that layer, select the frame that lines up with the last frame of the slideshow/animation.

4. **Insert | Timeline | Blank Key Frame** (*F7*).

5. With that new blank key frame selected, go to **Window | Actions** (*F9/Option F9*).

6. In the resulting Actions panel, type the following:

   ```
   this.stop();
   ```

   The code applies to `this` current timeline. It stops the animation at the frame the code is applied to. Merely typing stop(); is also adequate.

7. Save and test (*Ctrl/Cmmd Return*). The SWF should no longer loop. Make sure you like your last frame.

Swapping your slides

If you want to edit your timeline-based slideshow by changing the images in it, you can!

1. Open your slideshow file, if not already open.

2. Go to **File | Import | Import to Library**.

3. Import any image file(s) you need.

4. Select the key frame for the image you want to replace. This should in turn select the image.

5. Hit the **Swap** button in the Properties panel:

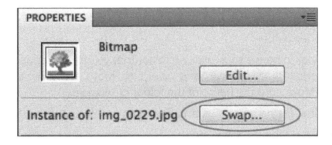

6. Select the image you want to use instead. Hit **OK**. The images are swapped.

7. Repeat as many times as necessary.

8. Save and test (*Ctrl/Cmmd Return*).

See also

▸ *Creating effects in Flash*

▸ *Using Flash to create watermarks*

▸ Chapter 9: *Flash Animations*

Building a slideshow in Flash with XML

The next level of creating elements in Flash is to incorporate XML. With XML, you do not have to open up Flash, import new image files into your FLA, and position them on the stage in the appropriate key frame. Instead, you can simply update your XML file in any text editor.

This method of slideshow creation is at the intermediate/advanced level because it requires a fair amount of ActionScript in your Flash document as well as an XML file. In addition to changing the images that display in the slideshow, the length of time they are displayed can be changed in the `.xml` file as well.

If you would like a preview of a sample slideshow, open the `slideshow_xml.fla` file in the `Chapter 3` folder.

Getting ready

Have images available to you and collected in one folder. JPG files will work well. It is usually best if the images have the same dimension. There are images available to you in the Chapter 3 images folder if you prefer that. You will also need access to a text editor, such as OpenOffice, to create the XML file.

How to do it...

1. Create a folder to house your `images` folder that you have prepped and your soon-to-be-created `.fla`, `.swf`, and `.xml` files. Move your `images` folder into this new folder. Make sure the name of the folder is `images`.

2. In a text editor, create a new file, and save it as `slideshow1.xml`.

3. In the `.xml` file, type the following:

    ```
    <?xml version="1.0" encoding="utf-8"?>
    <slideshow speed="4">
    <image picURL="images/pic01.jpg" />
    <image picURL="images/pic02.jpg" />
    <image picURL="images/pic03.jpg" />
    <image picURL="images/pic04.jpg" />
    <image picURL="images/pic05.jpg" />
    </slideshow>
    ```

4. Make sure that you use the name of your image files if they are not named `pic01.jpg`, etc., as in the example.

5. Save the `.xml` file to your folder that also contains your `images` folder.

6. Create a new file: File | New. Select Flash File (ActionScript 3.0)

7. Use **Modify** | **Page Properties** to set the Stage size as needed. Dimensions of 320 px wide by 240 px tall works well for the images in the `Chapter 3` folder.

8. Name **Layer 1** `actions`, and select the Key Frame.

9. Use **Window** | **Actions** or *F9/Option F9* to get the Actions panel. Insert the following code into the Actions panel for Frame 1 on the actions layer:

```
import fl.transitions.Tween;
import fl.transitions.easing.*;
import fl.transitions.TweenEvent;

var speed:Number;
var total:Number;
var pics:XMLList;

var loadersArray:Array=[];
var loadCounter:Number=0;
var playCounter:Number=0;

var slideshow:Sprite = new Sprite();
var picSlides:Sprite = new Sprite();

var timer:Timer;
var prevTween:Tween;
var tweenArray:Array=[];

var xml_loader:URLLoader = new URLLoader();
xml_loader.load(new URLRequest("slideshow1.xml"));
xml_loader.addEventListener(Event.COMPLETE, processXML);

function processXML(event:Event):void {
    var xml:XML=new XML(event.target.data);
    speed=xml.@Speed;
    pics=xml.image;
    total=pics.length();
    loadImages();
    xml_loader.removeEventListener(Event.COMPLETE, processXML);
    xml_loader=null;
}

function nextPic():void {
    var pic:Loader=Loader(loadersArray[playCounter]);
    picSlides.addChild(pic);
    pic.x = (stage.stageWidth - pic.width)/2;
    pic.y = (stage.stageHeight - pic.height)/2;
    tweenArray[0]=new Tween(pic,"alpha",Strong.easeOut,0,1,3,true);
}

function onFadeOut(event:TweenEvent):void {
    picSlides.removeChildAt(0);
}
```

```
function hidePrev():void {
    var pic:Loader=Loader(picSlides.getChildAt(0));
    prevTween=new Tween(pic,"alpha",Strong.easeOut,1,0,3,true);
    prevTween.addEventListener(TweenEvent.MOTION_FINISH,
onFadeOut);
}

function timerListener(event:TimerEvent):void {
    hidePrev();
    playCounter++;
    if (playCounter==total) {
        playCounter=0;
    }
    nextPic();
}

function startShow():void {
    addChild(slideshow);
    slideshow.addChild(picSlides);
    nextPic();
    timer=new Timer(speed*1000);
    timer.addEventListener(TimerEvent.TIMER, timerListener);
    timer.start();
}

function onComplete(event:Event):void {
    loadCounter++;
    if (loadCounter==total) {
        startShow();
    }
    var loaderInfo:LoaderInfo=LoaderInfo(event.target);
    loaderInfo.removeEventListener(Event.COMPLETE, onComplete);
}

function loadImages():void {
    for (var i:Number = 0; i < total; i++) {
        var url:String=pics[i].@picURL;
        var loader:Loader = new Loader();
        loader.load(new URLRequest(url));
        loader.contentLoaderInfo.addEventListener(Event.COMPLETE,
onComplete);
        loadersArray.push(loader);
    }
}
```

10. Save the file as `slideshow1.fla`.

11. Test the movie to generate the `.swf` file (*Ctrl/Cmd Return*).

How it works...

The `.swf` is populated by the images listed in the `.xml` file in the order in which they are listed. If you rearrange the order, you rearrange the order of the slideshow. If you change the images in the `.xml` list, you change the image that shows up in the `.swf`. This works because the ActionScript in the `.fla` calls the `.xml` file in this line of the code::

```
xml_loader.load(new URLRequest("slideshow1.xml"));
```

It uses a relative path to do this. So make sure that your `.swf` and `.xml` files are located as stated in your code.

In addition to controlling the order of the images, the `.xml` file also enables control over how long each image is visible:

```
<slideshow Speed="4">
```

If you change the number, you change the length of time an image shows up. Smaller numbers cause less time, larger numbers cause more time.

This ActionScript utilizes Sprites so that not even a Movie Clip symbol needs to be created on the stage. Positioning of the images happens based on the following lines of code that center it on the stage by dividing the stage dimensions by 2 to find the center:

```
picSlides.addChild(pic);
pic.x = (stage.stageWidth - pic.width)/2;
pic.y = (stage.stageHeight - pic.height)/2;
```

The fade effect is handled through an alpha change with a strong ease applied to it, as exemplified here:

```
tweenArray[0]=new Tween(pic,"alpha",Strong.easeOut,0,1,3,true);
```

There's more...

It is always possible to add more to a Flash file. By all means incorporate the information from the Flash watermarking recipe or your own design skills to continue to add visual elements to the `.fla`. Remember to make additional layers to hold the new elements if you are designing in the timeline.

In addition, if you would like to allow viewers to start and stop this slideshow, that is also possible. It does not even take very many more lines of code. You can check out the demo file to see this in action. It is the `slideshow_xml_buttons.fla` file in the `Chapter 3` folder. Below is a still from the slideshow:

Adding navigation (Start and Stop) buttons to the slideshow

All you have to do to add the ability to start and stop this slideshow is create a button for each function. Then, just add a few lines of code.

1. Use **Modify | Document** and increase the stage size. Since the code centers the images on the stage, increase the width and the height. `380 x 300 px` works well. More space is also fine, such as `550 x 400 px`.

2. Create a start button (see Chapter 9: *Creating buttons* if you need instructions on how to create a button symbol), and in the Properties panel, name the symbol instance on the stage `start_btn`.

3. Create a stop button, and in the Properties panel, name the symbol instance on the stage `stop_btn`.

4. Add the following lines of code to the end of your ActionScript in Flash:

```
function stopShow(event:MouseEvent):void{
    timer.stop();
}
```

```
function restartShow(event:MouseEvent):void{
    timer.start();
}

stop_btn.addEventListener(MouseEvent.CLICK, stopShow);
play_btn.addEventListener(MouseEvent.CLICK, restartShow);
```

5. Save the file as `slideshow_buttons.fla`, and test the movie (*Ctrl/Cmd Return*).

See also

▶   *Using Flash to create watermarks*

4
Video Blogging + Flash Video Encoding, Skinning, and Components

In this chapter, we will cover the following:

- ▶ FLV Embed plugin
- ▶ Video blogging using WebTV Plugin
- ▶ Video blogging using Free WP Tube theme
- ▶ Encoding with the Flash Media Encoder
- ▶ Using preset skins
- ▶ Hiding and Showing preset skins
- ▶ Using Video Component buttons
- ▶ Modifying Video Component buttons to customize your own skin

Introduction

Video is a major component of the Web today. Luckily, WordPress makes it easy to publish and share video. In this chapter, we will demonstrate ways of working with video in WordPress and in Flash. You will learn how to embed an .flv file, create an .xml video sitemap, and distribute your videos to sites such as YouTube and Blip. We will also show you how to set up Free WP Tube, a free video blogging theme that allows you to run a video web log (vlog).

Encoding through use of the Flash Media Encoder for reduced file sizes and creation of .flv is covered along with using Flash's default skinning options and editable Video components.

FLV Embed (Version 1.2.1)

If you want to embed .flv files, use a Flash video player, and/or publish a video sitemap, this compact plugin does all three. The homepage is http://www.channel-ai.com/blog/plugins/flv-embed/.

FLV Embed uses standards compliant, valid XHTML, and JavaScript. It is based on the JW FLV Media Player, whose homepage is http://www.longtailvideo.com/players/jw-flv-player/

FLV Embed supports Google video sitemap generation, allowing you to describe, syndicate, and distribute your video content, facilitating indexing in Google video search.

If a user is missing Flash or has disabled JavaScript, he or she is provided unobtrusive and appropriate on-screen instructions to correct the problem.

Getting ready

When a page with video loads, the player displays either the first frame of the video or a thumbnail (referred to as a poster image). The poster image is preferable, especially when a user is choosing between many videos—the first frame of a video may not offer the most representative or compelling description. Your poster image can be a poster or any image you like. Here is an example of our finished product:

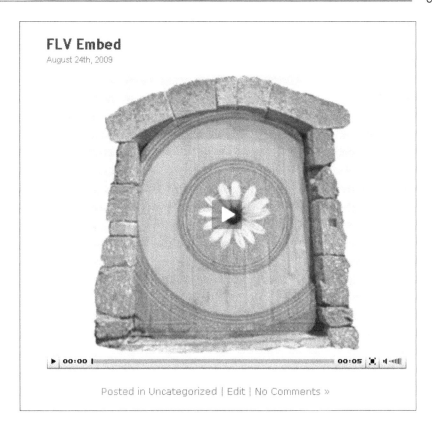

You will want to think about where you will upload the video files and poster images and, how you will name them. A good place might be `wp-content/uploads/video`.

This plugin requires that you name your poster images the same as your video files. The default image type is jpg, but you can use any valid image file format. All your images must be in the same file format.

A batch resize and rename utility is a useful tool. For PC, one free option is the Fast Stone Image Resizer, which you can download at `http://www.faststone.org/FSResizerDetail.htm`.

How to do it...

1. In your dashboard, navigate to **Plugins** | **Add New**. Search for "FLV Embed".
2. Click **Install,** then **Activate**.
3. Visit the plugin configuration panel at **Settings** | **FLV Embed.**

4. In the **Sitemap** menu, check the first box to **Enable sitemap feature and automatic custom field addition.** FLV Embed will now be able to create your video sitemap by automatically adding a custom field each time you use FLV Embed to insert a video.

5. In the **Poster** menu, check the box to **Display poster image for embedded FLV movies**.

6. For both of the fields, **Path to poster directory** and **Path to FLV directory**, we suggest you leave these blank, and instead use absolute URLs. If you do use relative (site-specific) URLs, keep in mind that a trailing slash is required. An example is `/wp-content/uploads/videos/`.

7. In the **Player** menu, you may want to change the colors or add your site logo as a linkable watermark to the video. Review all the **Settings**, and click **Save Changes**.

8. To embed an FLV file, use the following shortcode in HTML view: `[flv:url width height]`. For example, you could insert a YouTube video at 480 by 360 (using the absolute URL) like this:

   `[flv:http://youtube.com/watch?v=fLV3MB3DpWN 480 360]`

 A YouTube video cannot use a poster image because the file name of a jpg cannot contain a question mark.

9. You can also insert an FLV that you have uploaded (using the relative path) like this:

   `[flv:http://www.wordpressandflash.com/wp-content/uploads/video/ swfobject_test.swf 480 360]`

10. Once you have inserted the video, FLV Embed automatically populates the FLV custom field with two URLs, as you can see below. The first is the location of the video, and the second is the location of the poster image:

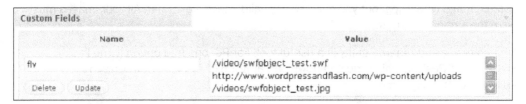

11. To use a custom poster image, upload any image to `wp-content/uploads/video`, and rename it to match the filename. You can also use an absolute URL if the poster image file is in another location—the filename must still match.

12. To configure your video XML sitemap, visit the **Video Sitemap Options** menu by clicking on **Settings | Video Sitemap**.

13. Here, you can get or modify the feed address. Our example is `http://www.wordpressandflash.com/ videofeed.xml`.

14. You can also adjust additional optional settings, and if you have made any changes to the settings or content and need to rebuild the sitemap or update your custom fields, you can do that here too.

How it works...

The video sitemap is an extension of the XML sitemap we explored in Chapter 2. A video sitemap allows you to publish and syndicate online video content, including descriptive metadata to tag your content for Google Video search. Adding details, such as a title and description, makes it easier for users who are searching to find a given piece of content. Your poster image will also be included as a clickable thumbnail image. The user will be directed to your website to see the video.

If FLV Embed cannot automatically generate the XML file, you can simply copy the XML file from the demo and save it to your server. Make sure to set the file permissions to write (664 or 666) by context-clicking in your FTP client and modifying the File Attributes, as seen below:

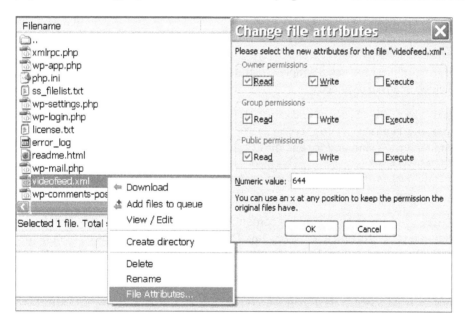

Then, make the appropriate changes to the **Video sitemap filename** field in the **Video Sitemap Options** menu, directing the plugin to the XML file you have prepared, and rebuild the sitemap.

Here is what your finished feed will look like:

There's more...

The `videofeed.xml` file has a simple structure. The first three tags specify encoding, styling, and the video sitemap protocol:

```
<?xml version="1.0" encoding="UTF-8"?>
<?xml-stylesheet type="text/xsl"
href="http://www.wordpressandflash.com/wp-content/plugins/flv-embed/
sitemap.xsl"?>
<urlset xmlns="http://www.sitemaps.org/schemas/sitemap/0.9"
        xmlns:video="http://www.google.com/schemas/sitemap-video/1.0">
```

Next, a `<url>` tag wraps each piece of content, which includes a `<loc>` tag (a link to the content on your site) and a `<video>` tag. The `<video>` tag contains additional tags that specify the video location, the video player location, the poster image location, a title, and description:

```
<url>
   <loc>http://www.wordpressandflash.com/flv-embed/</loc>
   <video:video>
        <video:content_loc>http://www.wordpressandflash.com/wp-
content/uploads/video/swfobject_test.swf</video:content_loc>
        <video:player_loc allow_embed="No">http://www.
wordpressandflash.com/wp-content/plugins/flv-embed/flvplayer.
swf?file=/wp-content/uploads/video/swfobject_test.swf</video:player_
loc>
        <video:thumbnail_loc>http://www.wordpressandflash.com/wp-
content/uploads/videos/swfobject_test.jpg</video:thumbnail_loc>
```

```
        <video:title><![CDATA[FLV Embed]]></video:title>
        <video:description><![CDATA[FLV Embed is a great plugin that
allows you to display FLV files &#8212; and most other video formats
&#8212; in a compact Flash video player.  Visit the homepage at:
http://www.channel-ai.com/blog/plugins/flv-embed/.  Check out the
video sitemap!
Get the latest Flash Player to see this player.
[Javascript required to view Flash movie, please turn it [...]]]></
video:description>
        </video:video>
</url>
</urlset>
```

With this info, you can manually create a `.xml` video feed for any site, without a plugin.

Commercial use?

Commercial use does require a license. A free alternative for commercial use is the Hana FLV Player, whose homepage is `http://www.neox.net/w/2008/05/25/hana-flv-player-wordpress-plugin/`.

See also

> ▸ Chapter 2: *Configuring WP for maximum SEO*

WebTV plugin (Version 0.6)

The WebTV Plugin, by Edgar de León, helps you distribute your video content. When you publish video using the WebTV plugin, the video will not only be published on your site, but it will be uploaded to a configurable list of popular distribution channels, including YouTube, Blip, and Vimeo.

The English language support page is `http://www.webstratega.com/webtv-wordpress-plugin-en/`.

How to do it...

1. In your dashboard, navigate to **Plugins | Add New**. Search for "WebTV."
2. Click **Install,** then **Activate**.
3. Visit the plugin configuration panel at **Settings | WebTV.**
4. Here, you will enter the username and password for each video distribution channel you want to use: YouTube, Vimeo, and Blip.tv.
5. Click **Save** to save your changes.

6. Create a new post by clicking **Posts | Add New.**

7. Give your post a title and put at least one word in the body. Under Publish (directly to the right of the title), click **Save Draft.**

8. Now, directly under the post body, look for the **WebTV Status** menu, shown below:

WebTV Status

Select Video (8 MB Max)

☐ Automatically publish post after one successful upload?

File Details:

9. Click on the blue button labeled **Select Video.**

10. **File Details** will show you the progress of the upload.

11. If you do not want to wait for the video to upload, put a check next to **Automatically publish post after one successful upload?**. Save your draft, and you can do something else—the post will go live once the video is ready.

There's more...

1. If you have trouble uploading video, the two most likely causes are the upload limit set by php.ini or file permissions.

2. If you need to increase the upload_max_filesize of your php.ini, contact your web hosting provider. If you are using a cpanel environment (such as bluehost, hostmonster, or hostgator), try the following:

3. Log in to your cpanel. In the Software/Services menu, click on **PHP Configuration**. Under **Install Default php.ini**, click **INSTALL PHP.INI MASTER FILE.**

4. This will create a copy of the master php.ini file to your public_html directory with the name of php.ini.default. Download the file via FTP. Then, edit the file name and contents. Search for upload_max_filesize and increase the value. Save your file as php.ini, and upload it to the directory in which WP is installed.

For how to change file permissions, see Chapter 4, *FLV Embed: How it works*. For security considerations, grant the minimum amount of access necessary: 644, 666, or 755.

See also

▶ Chapter 2: *Configuring WP for maximum SEO*

Free WP Tube (Version 1.0)

Free WP Tube is a free video blogging theme that uses custom fields to display videos and metadata. All you need is the embed code if the video is hosted on another site. You can also use the FLV Embed plugin to display video that you host inside a Flash video player. Free WP Tube is shown below:

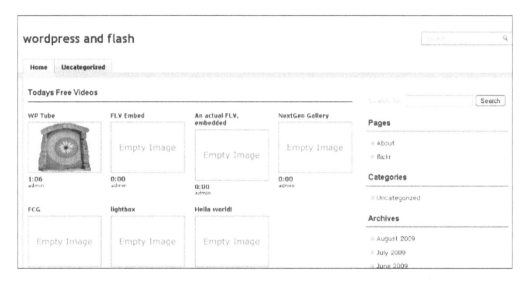

Download the installation package from `http://www.freewptube.com/`.

Getting ready

When you unzip the theme package, you will have a folder called **wptube**. Inside, find the folder named **plugins**. Free WP Tube is designed to use three plugins which are included in the zipped theme package:

- WP-PageNavi
- WP-PostViews
- WP-PostRatings

Upload these files to your `wp-content/plugins` folder, and activate each.

The entire `wptube` folder (minus the `plugins` folder) then need to be uploaded to `wp-content/themes`.

How to do it...

1. Activate the theme by clicking on **Appearance | Themes** and choosing the WP Tube theme.

2. Visit the theme configuration page. Look for a new menu at the bottom of your dashboard sidebar called **Tube Options**. There is only one option: **Show pages for menu?** Here, you decide whether or not to display pages, in addition to categories, in the top menu navigation.

3. Add a new post by clicking **Posts | Add New**.

4. Give your post a title, and enter some text in the post body. Assign a category as usual.

5. Scroll down to the custom fields menu. Three custom fields are required if you are inserting the embed code:

    ❑ **thumb** –The URL for the thumbnail image that will be shown on the homepage. The theme is designed to display an image size of 156x103 pixels. If you use a larger image, it will automatically be scaled to fit the predefined size. It is still worthwhile to resize (or batch resize) the thumbnail image(s) to the appropriate size, since the images will look better and the page will load faster.

    ❑ **duration** – The duration of the video.

    ❑ **video_code** – The embed code for the video.

6. If you want to post your own self-hosted video, use the shortcode in the post body for the FLV Embed plugin (see the first section of this chapter). In this case, do not include the `video_code custom` field. This figure shows the three required custom fields:

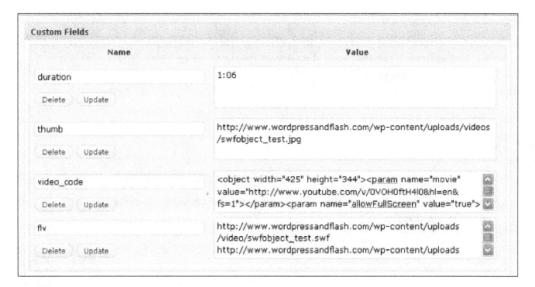

7. To control the number of videos displayed on the homepage, visit **Settings | Reading**, and enter your preferred number in the field **Blog pages show at most __ posts**.

More info

Another excellent and economical option for a video blogging is the eVid theme ($20) by Elegant themes: `http://www.elegantthemes.com/`.

See also

▶ *FLV Embed*

Encoding with the Adobe Media Encoder

If you have a video file, such as an MOV or MP4 file that you want to display as a SWF on the Web, simply encode (or compress) the video file into an FLV. With Flash CS4, you use the Adobe Media Encoder to do this. It can be accessed directly or through Flash's import video function. If you are using an earlier version of Flash, encoding is still possible, and the process is similar.

Getting ready

Make sure that you have a video file that is compatible with the Adobe Media Encoder. If you do not have a file to use, by all means, use the `short.mov` file in the `Chapter 4` folder. This file is a clip of the full length `summer.mp4` file from `www.archive.org` that is listed on that website as being in the Public Domain. Use the MOV file because it is a short file, so the time it takes the encoder to render the video will be shorter. This is good for the purposes of learning and practicing. Also, do not worry if you cannot hear any of the sounds. There is nothing wrong with the speakers on your computer. This file does not have audio.

How to do it...

1. Open the Adobe Media Encoder:

2. Click the **Add** button.

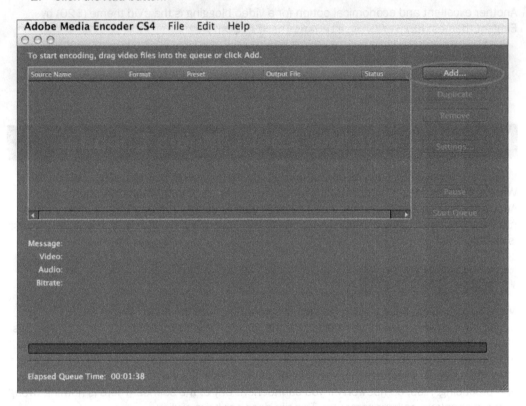

3. Navigate to the file you want to encode, such as short.move, and click **Choose/OK**.

    It is now listed in the queue:

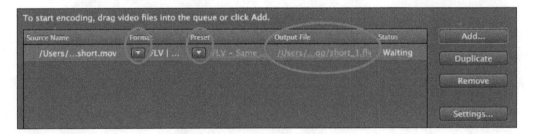

4. Click the down arrow under **Format** to select into which file format you will encode the video. Choose **FLV | F4V** if not already selected.

5. Click the down arrow under **Preset** to choose one of the preset export setting options. The default of **FLV - Same As Source (Flash 8 and Higher)** is generally fine. If you have fewer standard video needs, make a different choice based on your needs. Also, there is an option to **Edit Export Settings** as well as a **Settings** button if you want to make your own decisions. See the *Edit Export Settings* section for more on that.

6. Click on the file name under **Output File** to select the destination of your encoded file. You can also change the file name.

7. Click **Start Queue**, and the encoding process will begin. If you are encoding a long video, you might want to go take a walk or get a cup of tea. For short.mov, just sit tight. It should only take a minute or two to encode.

8. Once encoding is complete, the FLV is saved in the location you chose under the **Output File** section. There is also a check mark under the encoder's **Status** section. Now, you can do what you want with the file. For instance, you can take it into Flash and import it into an SWF.

How it works...

The Adobe Media Encoder encodes the selected video file into the FLV format. It is similar to taking a Photoshop file or a TIFF and compressing either of them into a JPG. The process is simply more involved because the data is more complex.

There's more...

The Adobe Media Encoder has many options and capabilities. Among these is a wealth of export settings that can be edited to suit your needs. Also available to you is the ability to not only encode multiple files in one sitting but also to duplicate and remove files in your queue.

Edit Export Settings

With your file selected in the encoder, click the **Settings** button. This gives you the **Export Settings** dialog box:

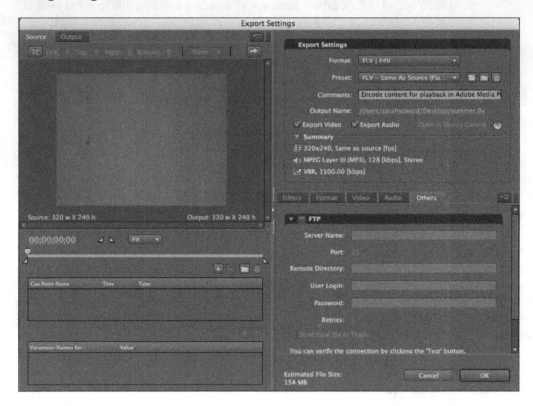

As you can see, it has a lot of options. The full purview of working with video for and in Flash is beyond the scope of this book. Only some of the myriad of options will be discussed below.

At the top left of the dialog box are two buttons: **Source** and **Output**. **Source** shows the video file you have selected. **Output** shows a preview of the encoded version of the file.

On the bottom/middle left of the **Export Settings** dialog box, you can address the timeline. You are able to clip the movie if you want to export only part of it; and you can set up cue points

To clip the movie, do the following:

1. Drag the playback head back and forth to manually preview the movie. This helps you find the section you want to keep.

2. Drag the in and out point triangles back and forth to isolate the section you want to keep. The triangle on the left is the in point, and the one on the right is the out point. Everything between the two triangles will be encoded.

The timer keeps track of time in milliseconds.

3. The right side of the dialog box allows you to change the desired file format; save your own preset with the button that looks like a computer disk circa 1996. You can also change the file name of the encoded video and choose if you are exporting only video, only audio, or both.

The **Summary** section gives you just that, a summary of your choices thus far.

The bottom right section gives you options for putting on a blur filter under the **Filter** tab and changing the format as applicable under the **Format** tab.

The **Video** tab lets you choose which **Codec** to use to encode the video. **On2 VP6** is usually the best choice. Stick with that one. It is more advanced, gives better quality, and allows you to encode an **Alpha Channel** if you have one to encode.

 Alpha Channels, areas of transparency in video (i.e., green screen), cannot be set up in Flash. They must be set up in a video editing program such as Premiere Pro or Final Cut Pro. The encoder can only honor them, not generate them.

If you need to resize your video, check the box for **Resize Video**, and change the values as needed. If you want to constrain the proportions of your video, leave the chain whole.

Frame rate can also be changed here. Generally, it is in your best interest to leave the video set to the same frame rate it was shot in. **Same as source** is a good choice. For **Bitrate Settings**, the defaults are usually pretty good. If you want higher quality and can take the additional file size, you can change **Encoding Passes** to **Two**.

For **Advanced Settings**, you can change overall quality by selecting either **Quality for Speed**, **Good**, or **Best**. It all depends on your needs.

For **Audio**, if you have it incorporated into your video file, choose **Stereo**. It sounds better. The only reason to go with **Mono** is if you have little sound, if it is a video of a talking head, or if your file size needs to be as small as possible.

For **Bitrate Settings** for audio, 128 kb per second is good. Again, only turn this lower if the audio is overly simple, not important, or your file size dictates it. Faster bitrate/higher number gives you better quality sound.

When you are finished making changes, click **OK**. This gets you back to the encoder. Proceed from here as needed.

Encoding multiple files at once

This is a piece of cake. If you want to encode more than one file in a row, you absolutely can!

1. Click the **Add** button in the Adobe Media Encoder to add another file. In the **Open** dialog box, select the file—or *Shift Click* to select multiple files—and hit **Open**. Do this as many times as necessary to get all of the files you want to encode into your queue.

2. Once the files are in the queue, change the format, preset, and output file name as needed.

3. Click **Start Queue**. Flash starts at the top of the queue and works its way down one file at a time.

This is also useful if you want to encode the same file with different settings to compare the quality, etc. For this, select the file that you want to test, and click **Duplicate** as many times as you need. Change the **Preset**, or click **Settings** as needed for each copy of the file. When you are ready, click **Start Queue**.

Removing files

1. Select one file or more in the queue.

2. Click **Remove**.

    You will get the following dialog box:

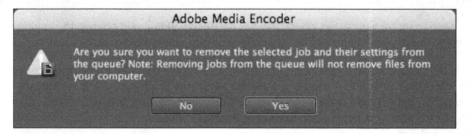

3. Click **Yes**. Ta-Dah!

Files can be removed from the queue regardless of their status as either **Waiting** or complete.

See also

▸ *Embedding Flash as .swf pb-embedFlash/Kimili plugin*

▸ *Embedding Flash as .flv FLV-Embed plugin*

▸ *Using preset skins*

▸ Using Video Component buttons to customize your skin

Using preset skins

After you encode an FLV file, you can import it into Flash and use a preset skin to allow you and your viewers to control the finished product. Flash's preset skins consist of a rounded corner rectangle for a background panel and any of a number of different buttons. The design for these default skins is the same inside each type; only the kind and number of buttons changes. There are two types of preset skins: skins that show up over the top of your video and skins that show up under your video. Choose the one with the buttons you need. There are options for basics like play/pause and mute, as well as more advanced buttons to enable full screen mode and closed captions. Color can also be affected.

Getting ready

Make sure that you have access to an FLV file. If you completed the recipe for encoding with the Adobe Media Encoder, you can use that FLV. If you need an FLV file, use short.flv from the Chapter 4 folder.

How to do it...

1. In Flash, create a new file by going to **File | New** (*Cmd/Ctrl N*). Select Flash File (ActionScript 3.0), and hit **OK**.

2. Go to **File | Import | Import Video**. You should get the following dialog box:

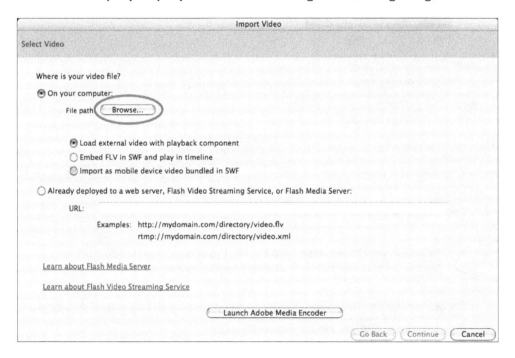

3. Click **Browse**, navigate to the video file of your choice (such as `short.flv`), and hit **Choose/OK**.

 If you forgot to encode your video file as an `FLV` before attempting to import it, click on the **Launch Adobe Media Encoder** button. This opens the encoder so that you can remedy your forgetfulness. Once encoding is complete, just go back into Flash, click **OK** if you get a warning dialog box, and browse to your `FLV`.

4. Leave **Load external video with playback component** selected. This is the best choice if sound is involved in your video and also helps with load time.

5. Click **Continue** to get the following options for skinning your `FLV`:

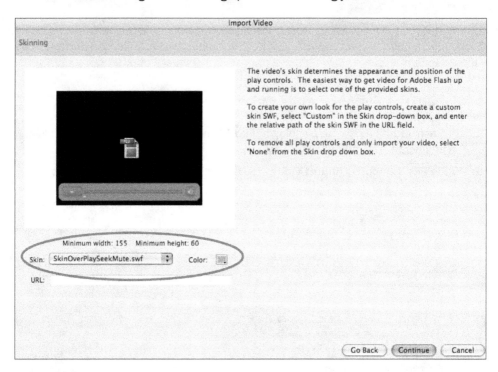

6. Choose any skin you want/like/need.

 You can also choose **None** from the list if you do not want to use a preset skin but would prefer either none at all or to make your own.

7. Choose a color for the skin by clicking on the color swatch to access the color picker.

8. Click **Continue**, and you get the **Summary** page.

9. Click **Finish**, and give Flash a moment to generate everything necessary on the stage.

This is what shows up in Flash:

10. Save the file (*Cmd/Ctrl S*), and test the movie (*Cmd/Ctrl Return*) to generate the SWF and see the file in action.

You now have your FLV, the SWF file of your movie, and a SWF file of your skin. You will need to bring all of these pieces into WordPress for the movie to play accurately.

How it works...

The Adobe Media Encoder encodes the selected video file into the FLV format. The FLV file format is highly compatible with the Adobe Flash Player and is generally a small file size for video. Once FLV encoding is complete, the **Import Video** function of Flash imports the FLV into Flash and wraps it inside an SWF when you test or publish your Flash movie. If you choose a skin, Flash also generates an SWF file for the skin. The buttons in the skin are coded and pretty much ready to go. Some of the more advanced buttons, like the one for full screen mode, require a little more effort on your part. See the section on *Setting up Fullscreen mode* below.

You get all of this functionality without typing a single line of code.

There's more...

The different buttons available in the preset skins have different capabilities. Choosing different buttons allows your viewer to interact with your movie to varying degrees. Some of the default settings for the movie can be changed using the Component Inspector panel. Below are a few suggestions for ways to edit the default settings.

Hiding and showing preset skins

Just because you chose a skin, it does not mean that you always want it to be visible. Flash has settings to allow you to hide and show your chosen skin If you want to hide/show your skin, use the following steps:

1. In Flash, have a file open that has a preset skin. If you do not have a file, use `skinning.fla` from the `Chapter 4` folder.

2. Use the Selection Tool to select the FLVPlayback component on the stage.

3. Go to **Window | Component Inspector** if it is not already open:

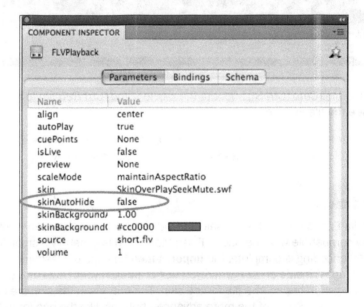

4. Make sure that **Parameters** is selected at the top of the panel. This panel allows you to change settings for the FLVPlayback component skin without messing around with code. There are a number of things you can change.

5. To allow the skin to hide when the viewer's mouse is not over the movie and show when the mouse is over the movie, click on the word **false** to the right of **skinAutoHide**. Change **false** to **true**.

6. Test the movie (*Cmd/Ctrl Return*), and move your cursor over and away from the movie to see hide and show in action.

Stopping AutoPlay

If you want your movie to load in the stopped position, rather than playing as soon as it loads, do the following:

1. In Flash, have a file open that has a preset skin. If you do not have a file, use `skinning.fla` from the `Chapter 4` folder.

2. Use the Selection Tool to select the FLVPlayback component.

3. Go to **Window | Component Inspector** if it is not already open:

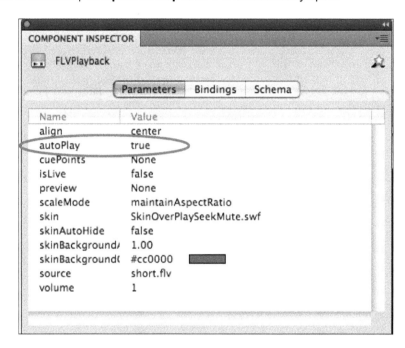

4. Make sure that **Parameters** is selected at the top of the panel.

5. Click on the word **true** to the right of **autoPlay**. Change **true** to **false**.

6. Test the movie (*Cmd/Ctrl Return*) to check that it does not automatically start playing. The viewer must hit the play button to get the movie to play.

Setting up Fullscreen mode through Flash

By default, fullscreen mode is enabled in the SWF. In order for it to work, however, you need to add some code to your PHP file in WordPress that will hold the SWF. Follow with us as we go through the necessary steps:

1. In Flash, have a file open that has a preset skin with the fullscreen button on it. If you do not have a file, use skinning.fla from the Chapter 4 folder.

2. Go to **File | Publish Settings:**

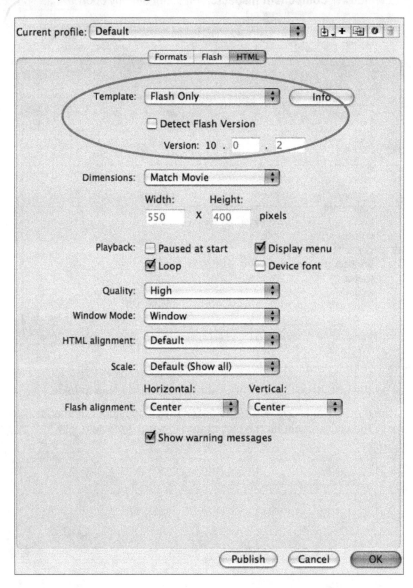

3. Select the **HTML** tab to see the settings.

4. For **Template**, select **Flash Only - Allow Fullscreen Mode**.

5. Check the box for **Detect Flash Version**; for **Version**, set it to at least **9.0.28**. It can also be set to a later version of the Flash player.

6. Click **Publish** to generate the HTML page with the necessary code.

7. Preview this page in your browser by double clicking the HTML file. This is just to make sure it is working.

 According to Adobe, you will need Flash Player version 9.0.28 or later for the fullscreen mode to work.

8. View the code for the HTML file. This is easily done by going to **View** | **Page Source** (or something similar) when the file is open in your browser. There should be JavaScript in the <head> section and the <body> section. This needs to be copied and pasted into your WordPress file that is going to house your SWF.

The code in the <head> section is quite lengthy, so it is reproduced here only in part. Copy all of the JavaScript elements in the <head> of the HTML file to the <head> of your file in WordPress. The code begins and ends as follows (the middle is not included due to its length. Also, there may be some differences in your code depending on settings, etc.):

```
<script language="JavaScript" type="text/javascript">
<!--
//v1.7
// Flash Player Version Detection
// Detect Client Browser type
// Copyright 2005-2008 Adobe Systems Incorporated.  All rights
reserved.
var isIE  = (navigator.appVersion.indexOf("MSIE") != -1) ? true :
false;
var isWin = (navigator.appVersion.toLowerCase().indexOf("win") != -1)
? true : false;

-------- code excerpted due to length --------

      case "class":
      case "title":
      case "accesskey":
      case "name":
      case "tabindex":
        ret.embedAttrs[args[i]] = ret.objAttrs[args[i]] = args[i+1];
        break;
      default:
        ret.embedAttrs[args[i]] = ret.params[args[i]] = args[i+1];
```

```
      }
    }
    ret.objAttrs["classid"] = classid;
    if (mimeType) ret.embedAttrs["type"] = mimeType;
    return ret;
}
// -->
</script>
<script language="JavaScript" type="text/javascript">
<!--
// -----------------------------------------------------------------
-----------
// Globals
// Major version of Flash required
var requiredMajorVersion = 9;
// Minor version of Flash required
var requiredMinorVersion = 0;
// Revision of Flash required
var requiredRevision = 28;
// -----------------------------------------------------------------
-----------
// -->
</script>
```

The `<body>` section code, similar to what is below, needs to be pasted into the `<body>` of your file in WordPress and should look something like this:

```
<script language="JavaScript" type="text/javascript">
<!--
var hasRightVersion = DetectFlashVer(requiredMajorVersion,
requiredMinorVersion, requiredRevision);
if(hasRightVersion) {  // if we've detected an acceptable version
    // embed the flash movie
    AC_FL_RunContent(
        'codebase', 'http://download.macromedia.com/pub/shockwave/cabs/
flash/swflash.cab#version=9,0,28,0',
        'width', '550',
        'height', '400',
        'src', 'skinning',
        'quality', 'high',
        'pluginspage', 'http://www.adobe.com/go/getflashplayer',
        'align', 'middle',
        'play', 'true',
        'loop', 'true',
        'scale', 'showall',
```

```
            'wmode', 'window',
            'devicefont', 'false',
            'id', 'skinning',
            'bgcolor', '#ffffff',
            'name', 'skinning',
            'menu', 'true',
            'allowFullScreen', 'true',
            'allowScriptAccess','sameDomain',
            'movie', 'skinning',
            'salign', ''
            ); //end AC code
} else {  // flash is too old or we can't detect the plugin
    var alternateContent = 'Alternate HTML content should be placed
here.'
        + 'This content requires the Adobe Flash Player.'
        + '<a href="http://www.adobe.com/go/getflashplayer/">Get Flash</
a>';
    document.write(alternateContent);  // insert non-flash content
}
// -->
</script>
<noscript>
    // Provide alternate content for browsers that do not support
scripting
    // or for those that have scripting disabled.
        Alternate HTML content should be placed here. This content
requires the Adobe Flash Player.
        <a href="http://www.adobe.com/go/getflashplayer/">Get Flash</a>

</noscript>
```

Only incorporate the code inside the `<script> </script>` and `<noscript> </noscript>` tags for each sections. The two sections of code work together to allow fullscreen mode to function properly in different browsers.

See also

▶ *Embedding Flash as .swf pb-embedFlash/Kimili plugin*

▶ *Encoding with the Adobe Media Encoder*

▶ Using Video Component buttons to customize your skin

Using Video Component buttons to customize your skin

It is possible that you might prefer to make a skin look the way *you* want it to look, rather than the way that Adobe designed it to look. There are ways to make this happen. In addition to the preset skins used in previous recipes, you can also use individual component buttons to customize your skin.

Getting ready

Make sure that you have access to an FLV file. If you completed the recipe for *Encoding with the Adobe Media Encoder*, you can use that FLV. If you need an FLV file, use short.flv from the Chapter 4 folder.

How to do it...

1. In Flash, create a new file by going to **File | New** (*Cmd/Ctrl N*).

2. Select **Flash File (ActionScript 3.0)**, and hit **OK**.

3. Go to **File | Import | Import Video**.

4. Click **Browse**, navigate to the video file of your choice (such as short.flv), and hit **Choose/OK**.

5. Leave **Load external video with playback component** selected. This is the best choice if sound is involved in your video and also helps with load time.

6. Click **Continue**, to get the options for skinning your FLV. For **Skin**, choose **None**.

7. Click **Continue**, and you get the summary page.

8. Click **Finish**, and give Flash a moment to import the file to the stage.

9. If the **Components** panel is not already open, go to **Window | Components**. Click on the triangle next to **Video**, as shown in the following screenshot, to get the full list of preset **Video** components that you can use and ultimately alter:

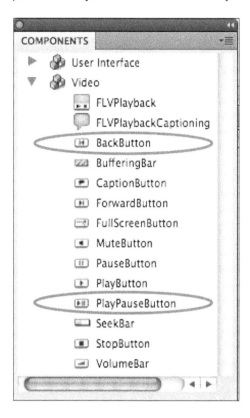

10. To use any one of the component buttons, simply drag it from the **Components** panel onto the stage. Place it where you want it. It can be on top of, below, or beside your FLV. Unlike with the preset skin, you get to choose the placement.

If you want more control over placement, create a new layer for the components. Also, you can create a layer below the components and design a panel for the components to sit on. The panel can be as simple as the rounded corner rectangle of the preset skins or more complex with opacity settings and gradation. It is up to you!

11. As an example, drag the **PlayPauseButton** onto the stage, and test your movie (*Cmd/ Ctrl Return*). Click the button in the SWF. It toggles between being a pause button when the movie is playing and a play button when the movie is paused.

12. Go back into Flash and drag out the **BackButton**. Test the movie (*Cmd/Ctrl Return*). Click on this button to jump back to the start of the movie.

How it works...

These components are pre-coded and ready to go. All you have to do to get the video components to work is have one FLV on the stage for them to affect. The components take care of the rest themselves.

There's more...

Want more diversity in your design? Check out the next section on editing the look of the component buttons.

Modifying Video Component buttons for further customization

The components can be visually altered to make your FLV player even more individualized and unique.

Very simply, you can use the Transform Tool to change the size of the component. Just select a component with the Free Transform Tool, and drag the bounding box to make the component larger or smaller.

The components are movie clip symbols, so you can use the **Properties** panel to apply a **Color Effect**. Select the component(s) you want to change, choose a **Style** of **Color Effect**, and change the settings for that **Color Effect**. The selected component(s) will be affected.

Less simply, you can edit the parts of the component discretely. These are movie clip symbols. You can double click on the symbol instance on the stage or double click on the icon for the symbol in the **Library** to edit the symbol.

Do not delete the symbols that make up the component. This can break the component. If you do not want part of a component to be visible and if it is a symbol itself, then lower the opacity of that symbol instance. Do not delete the symbol instance(s) inside the component.

To reduce confusion, this section uses one of the components with a simpler design: the **BackButton**. Also, to keep things simpler, the symbols that make up the **BackButton** component are going to be accessed through the **Library** panel and referred to by the name that is applied by default, as we see below:

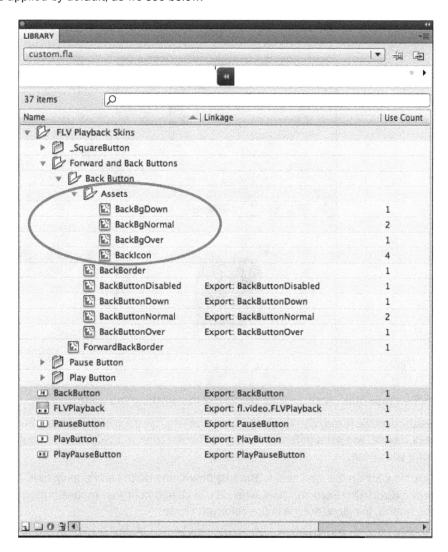

1. The **Library** should have a folder called **FLV Playback Skins**. Click on the triangle next to that folder to open it. It holds all the pieces that make up the different video components that you placed on the stage.

2. Open the folder for the **Forward and Back Buttons** and for the **Back Button** to gain access to the pieces of the **BackButton** component.

3. The **Back Button** folder contains a folder of **Assets** that are used in the other movie clip symbols outside the **Assets** folder. Start by editing the elements in the **Assets** folder.

4. For instance, *double click* on the icon next to **BackBgOver** to change the look of the background elements of the rollover state, such as the color of the glow. In the **Timeline**, click on the keyframe for the **Glow** layer to select the outer glow:

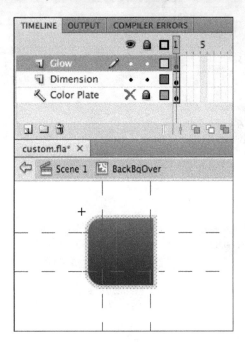

5. In the **Properties** panel, change the fill color to anything you want.

6. Test the movie (*Cmd/Ctrl Return*) to see that when you roll over the back button with your mouse, you get a different color glow/border than you did before. You get the color you chose.

7. *Double click* on the icon beside **BackBgDown**, and do the same thing to it. Test the movie (*Cmd/Ctrl Return*). Now, when you click and hold your mouse button down on the button, the glow/outline is the color you chose.

8. *Double click* on **BackIcon** to change the look of the double arrows on the button. Make them larger or smaller with the Transform Tool, or change their color. Since this icon inside of the movie clip symbol is just a merged shape, you can delete this and replace it with something else.

You can even add more layers to any of the movie clips that make up the component. Just do not delete any of the movie clip symbols on the stage or in the library!

See also

▶ *Encoding with the Adobe Media Encoder*

▶ Using preset skins

5

Working with Audio— Using Plugins and Flash

In this chapter, we will cover the following:

- ▶ Using the WPAudio Player plugin
- ▶ Using the µAudio plugin
- ▶ Using the PodPress plugin
- ▶ Using buttons in the Common Library
- ▶ Adding sound effects to a button
- ▶ Adding sound effects to the timeline
- ▶ Streaming sound and coding a simple on/off music button
- ▶ Designing your own stylish MP3 player
- ▶ Coding your own stylish MP3 player

Introduction

In this chapter, we show you how to work with audio in WordPress and in Flash. Topics that we will cover include using a Flash audio player plugin and creating a podcast. In addition, you will also learn how to use pre-made buttons from Flash's Common Library in preparation for creating your own music/sound file control buttons. You will also learn how to incorporate sound files in different ways in Flash so that you can have more personalized audio features on your blog.

Any SWF file can be imported into WordPress. Just remember that if you are loading external files into an SWF, those files also need to be uploaded.

WPAudio Player plugin (Version 1.5.2)

WPAudio is a plugin for WordPress that embeds a Flash audio player through the use of shortcode. It is compact and easy to use. Based on a JavaScript sound API called SoundManager2, it uses JavaScript and Flash. The homepage of SoundManager2 is `http://www.schillmania.com/projects/soundmanager2/`, and the homepage of WPAudio is `http://wpaudio.com/`.

How to do it...

1. Download and install the plugin by going to **Plugins | Add New**, and search for "WPAudio."

2. Click **Install** and **Activate**.

3. Add a new post by clicking **Post** and **Add New**.

4. To upload your audio file, use FTP. Another option is to use the built-in audio browser uploader. Look for the musical note icon above the Visual Editor, the third button to the right of **Upload/Insert**, circled in the example below:

5. Browse to the file on your computer and upload (as shown in the following screenshot). Once complete, copy the **Link URL** field to get the address of the file. Do not click **Insert into Post** (since doing so will simply insert a link to your .mp3 file, and our goal is to use the WPAudio player)—simply click the "X" on the top right to close the window.

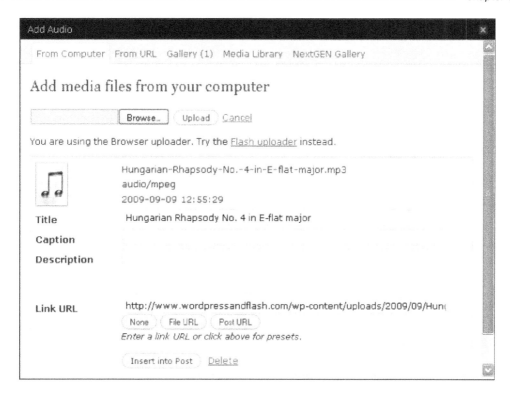

6. Now, we can add our shortcode, [wpaudio]. The one required parameter is url.

    ```
    [wpaudio url="http://www.wordpressandflash.com/wp-content/
    uploads/Hungarian Rhapsody No. 4 in E-flat major.mp3"]
    ```

There's more...

To change the colors used in the player, visit the plugin configuration page at **Settings | Wpaudio**. The **Style** menu allows you to customize the colors.

If you do not want the file name to be the title on the player, you can specify alternate text using the text parameter, like in the following:

```
[wpaudio url="http://www.wordpressandflash.com/wp-content/uploads/
Hungarian Rhapsody No. 4 in E-flat major.mp3" text="Hungarian
Rhapsody No. 4 in E-flat major composed by Franz Liszt and
performed by Vadim Chaimovich on Keyboard, from musopen.com"]
```

You can specify an alternate download location by using the `dl` parameter:

```
[wpaudio url="http://www.wordpressandflash.com/wp-content/uploads/
Hungarian Rhapsody No. 4 in E-flat major.mp3" dl="http://www.
musopen.com/music.php?type=piece&id=249"]
```

You can disable the download option by setting `dl` to "0":

```
[wpaudio url="http://www.wordpressandflash.com/wp-content/uploads/
Hungarian Rhapsody No. 4 in E-flat major.mp3" dl="0"]
```

µAudio plugin (Version 0.6.2)

µAudio, or MicroAudio, is an ultra compact (6kb) Flash mp3 player that appears each time a `.mp3` link is clicked on your site. It uses your existing CSS styling, so it will cleanly integrate into most themes automatically. You can modify the existing CSS or write custom rules. Simple to install and use, µAudio is an excellent solution for playing `.mp3` files in a WordPress site.

µAudio is authored by Christopher O'Connell. The plugin homepage is `http://compu.terlicio.us/code/plugins/audio/`.

µAudio is based on the 1 Pixel Out player and requires jQuery 1.3. The 1 Pixel Out plugin homepage is `http://www.1pixelout.net/code/audio-player-wordpress-plugin/`

How to do it...

1. Download, install, and activate the plugin.

2. Visit the plugin configuration page by clicking on **Settings | µAudio**.

3. The **jQuery** box should remain checked unless you are already loading jQuery 1.3 or later in your header.

4. Use **Autostart** with discretion so as to not offend your visitors. We suggest you keep this box unchecked.

5. If you would like to use the µAudio player in your sidebar, check the **Enable Sidebar Widget** box.

6. The **Configuration** menu allows you to choose between three options: using the default player, using existing CSS, or using `microAudio.example.css` (a custom class you must overwrite or add to your stylesheet). Make the appropriate selection.

7. Check the box next to **Download Link**. This will give users the option to download the file they are listening to.

8. Click **Configureate** to save your changes.

9. To use the plugin, create a new post (page or text widget). Simply create a link to your mp3 file. Our example is `<a href="http://www.wordpressandflash.com/wp-content/uploads/Hungarian Rhapsody No. 4 in E-flat major.mp3">please listen to this excellent mp3!</a>`

10. The finished result looks like this:

There's more...

It is very easy to adjust the CSS styling for µAudio. The first step is to choose the colors you want and generate the hex triplet values using Photoshop, GIMP, or an online list such as `http://en.wikipedia.org/wiki/Web_colours#X11_color_names`.

Connect to your site via FTP, and navigate to the following directory: `wp-content/plugins/microaudio`.

Download the file named `microAudio.example.css`.

Open up `microAudio.example.css` in a text editor such as Notepad ++.

Make changes to the style sheet definitions (color and width) as appropriate.

CSS Basics

Make sure to preserve the correct CSS syntax:

`.selector {property: value;}`

Each selector is either a class, starting with a period (`.`), an ID, starting with the pound sign (#), or a HTML tag, such as h1 (for the `<h1>` or heading 1 tag) or p (for the `<p>` or paragraph tag). A class or ID must be followed (without any space) by a unique name. The properties must be wrapped in curly braces (`{}`). Each property is followed by a colon (`:`), and each value should end with a semi-colon (`;`).

In this example, we change line 19 of `microAudio.example.css` to change the background color to fern green:

```
.microAudio-bg {
    color: #4F7942;
    }
```

You can change the width by adjusting the `mAp, .adplr` class on line 139:

```
.mAp, .adplr {
    width: 300px;
    }
```

PodPress plugin (Version 8.8.1)

PodPress is an excellent solution for bloggers who want to share their audio (or video) content as an RSS feed or podcast. PodPress is both a Flash media player and a content syndication tool—so, you can easily embed audio in a post or page and distribute it to podcast directories such as iTunes, Yahoo! Podcasts, Podcast Alley, Podcastready, and blubrry. Other features include a custom image for videos, a custom image for your feed, and download statistics.

The PodPress homepage is `http://www.mightyseek.com/podpress`.

PodPress is based upon the 1 Pixel Out Flash media player (same as the µAudio plugin) and WP-iPodCatter plugin. The homepage of WP-iPodCatter is `http://garrickvanburen.com/wordpress-plugins/wpipodcatter`.

How to do it...

1. Download and install the plugin by going to **Plugins | Add New.** Search for "PodPress."

2. Click **Install** and **Activate**.

3. Add a new post by clicking **Post | Add New**. Below the post body you will see a new menu for podcasting, like this example shows:

4. Here, you enter the URL of the audio or video file in the **Location** field. An unlimited number of files can be attached—click **Add Media File** to add more.

5. Add a title. (This is optional, but suggested.)

6. The **Type** should be automatically recognized. If not, use the pull-down menu to make the appropriate selection.

7. Click **Auto Detect for Size and Duration**, or enter these manually.

8. You should not have to disable the player—PodPress is compatible with all standard media formats, including MP3, MP4, OGG, MOV, FLV, SWF, ASF, WMV, AVI, and YouTube.

9. Now, all you have to do is insert the player in your post, using shortcode:
    ```
    [display_podcast]
    ```

10. Visit the plugin configuration page by clicking on the **PodPress** menu in the dashboard sidebar. Then, click on **Feed/iTunes Settings**.

11. Under the **Standard Settings,** you will want to note the address of your podcast feed. This is automatically generated by PodPress. Our example is `http://www.wordpressandflash.com/?feed=podcast`.

12. Here is how your finished feed will look:

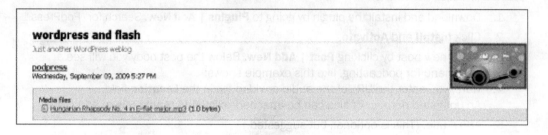

13. You may also want to specify an image for your podcast feed in the **Blog/RSS Image** field. 144 by 144 pixels is the best size.

14. To access the menus for each of the podcast directories, click on the appropriate logo at top. Then, you can set up your feed for each directory you intend to use, like this example shows:.

15. Visit the **PodPress | General Settings**.

16. Here, you can enable statistics by checking the box **Enable PodPress Statistics**.

17. You might also want to remove the image by using the pull-down menu to select **None** for the **Image** field. See above for the PodPress player—the image is the part that says **Audio MP3**. This could be redundant in many scenarios. Below we see part of this removal process:

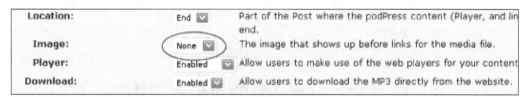

18 Click **Update Settings** to save your changes.

19. Visit the player settings by clicking on **PodPress** | **Player Settings**.

20. Here, you can switch between the two available players, customize the colors of the selected player, or set the default image for video files.

21. Click **Update Options** to save your changes.

22. Once you have enabled statistics, visit the **PodPress** | **Stats** menu to review.

There's more...

In our test environment, we used PodPress 8.81 and WordPress 2.7 without any problem. There have been reports of problems for some users with WP 2.6 and 2.7. A patch is available. See the WP forums for more information: `http://wordpress.org/support/topic/225639`.

Using buttons in the Common Library

This technical recipe is in preparation for the following music-oriented recipes. It is written for people who are not very familiar with Flash but still want to be able to accomplish the next few recipes. Here you will learn how to use pre-made buttons from Flash's Common Library. It is really very simple.

How to do it...

1. In Flash, create a new file by going to **File** | **New** (*Cmd/Ctrl N*). Select **Flash File (ActionScript 3.0)**, and hit **OK**.

2. Go to **Window** | **Common Libraries** | **Buttons**, and a panel will appear that has a lot of folders in it. Each folder holds different buttons and the pieces (assets) that make up those buttons:

3. Click on one of the triangles to the left of a folder to open the folder. For buttons that look like play, stop, fast forward, and the like, choose a folder with **playback** as part of its name.

4. Click on the different buttons inside the folder to see what each looks like in the preview window at the top of the panel. There is a tiny play button in the top right of the panel that you can click to see the different states (up, over, down) of the button. They play quickly.

5. Once you find a button you like, drag it onto the stage where you want it to show up. You can drag it out by its name in the list or by the image in the preview window.

6. To resize the button, if you want to, make sure it is selected, and change the width and height, **W:** and **H:**, in the **Properties** panel.

7. Save the file (*Ctrl/Cmd S*), and test the movie (*Ctrl/Cmd Return*). While testing the movie, roll your mouse over the button to see the over state, and click on the button to see the down state.

You now have a button that is ready to have ActionScript applied to it!

How it works...

Flash offers a number of pre-made elements that are easy to use. The buttons in the Common Library do not come with code attached. They do, however, come with rollover and down states ready to go. All you have to do is drag a button out of the Common Library and onto the stage to use it. It is very similar to creating your own assets and storing them in the Library for reuse later. In fact, when you drag a button onto the stage from the Common Library, it gets added into your Library for easy reuse later.

There's more...

What if you like a button, but you are not crazy about the look of the over state? Can the different states of the buttons be edited? You betcha! It is all a matter of double clicking.

Editing a button from the Common Library

1. *Double click* on either the symbol instance of your button on the stage or on the symbol in the **Library** to isolate the button and access its user-based timeline.

   The timeline for the button symbol instance should look something like this:

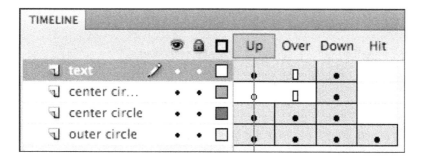

2. You may have more or fewer layers depending on the complexity of the button you chose. The important thing is that something appears in at least one layer for each of the four states: **Up, Over, Down, Hit**. This ensures that the button is visible at all times and will function properly with an adequately sized **Hit** state (the active area of the button).

3. To see each of the different states, move the red playback head over each state. No one ever sees your **Hit** state. It does not matter what it looks like. It only matters that it is large enough for a person to hit with a mouse.

4. To edit something, click on it. Either click on the key frame in the timeline or on the object on the stage.

5. From here, you can change the scale, color, rotation, and more of any part of the button. You can delete elements and also draw or import more. It is up to you. Enjoy!

See also

▸ *Designing your own button*

▸ *Creating a complex button*

Adding sound effects to a button

To increase user feedback, you can add sound effects to a button. Sound effects are most useful when applied to either the **Over** or **Down** state. We recommend putting sound effects only on the **Down** state so that users hear the sound when they successfully click on the button rather than every single time they roll over it—on purpose or accidentally. If you are doing game design or creating applications for children, for instance, your priorities may be different from ours. The process is the same for placing a sound effect on either state; it is just a matter of selecting that state in the timeline.

Getting ready

Have a Flash file open that has a button symbol on it.

How to do it...

1. Make sure the sound is turned on for your computer.

2. Double click on the button symbol instance on the stage or the button symbol in the library to isolate the button and its timeline.

3. Click the new layer button at the bottom left of the timeline to create a new layer.

4. *Double click* on the name of this layer, and rename it **sound effect**.

5. Drag this layer to the top of the timeline.

6. Click on the frame for the **Down** state so that it is highlighted:

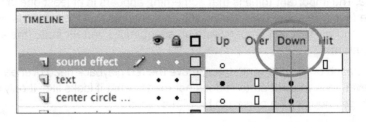

7. Hit *F6* to create a new key frame that will hold the sound effect.

8. Go to **Window | Common Library | Sounds** to pull out the menu of default sounds that come with Flash. You get a panel full of different sound effects of varying lengths:

9. Click on a sound to select it. Then, hit the play button in the top right corner of the preview window to hear the sound. For the purposes of a button, try a short sound.

You are not limited to the sound files that Flash has available in this library. You can go to **File | Import | Import to Library** and choose a compatible sound file from your own source. You can then use that sound file/library item in the same way as the sound files from the Common Library.

10. With the key frame for the **Down** state on the sound effect layer selected, drag the sound onto the stage. Either drag the item from the list or the wavelength from the preview window.

Nothing will show up on the stage because sound is not visible to the human eye. However, a wavelength representation will show up in the key frame in the timeline.

11. Save the file (*Ctrl/Cmd S*), and test the movie (*Ctrl/Cmd Return*). While testing the movie, roll your mouse over the button to see the over state, and click on the button to see **and hear** the down state.

How it works...

Sound can be added to a key frame just as an image can. The sound effect gets stored in the Library of the file and accessed/played when a user performs the appropriate action. In this case, a user just needs to click on the button to hear the sound.

There's more...

If you need sound when you roll your mouse over the button, you can add sound to the **Over** state.

Adding sound to the Over state

If you need a sound effect on the **Over** state instead of, or as well as, on the **Down** state, simply follow the directions above with one difference. The key frame goes on the frame for the **Over** state rather than the **Down** state.

Everything else is the same.

See also

▸ *Using buttons in the Common Library*

▸ *Designing your own button*

▸ *Creating a complex button*

▸ *Adding sound effects to the timeline*

Adding sound effects to the timeline

When you want the sound to happen at a specific time in your movie rather than when a user performs a specific action (like clicking on a button), put the sound effect into the time-based timeline. Sound effects can go into the main timeline and into the timelines of movie clips just as they can into the timelines of buttons. In this recipe, you will learn how to put a sound effect into a time-based timeline.

Getting ready

Have a file open into which you want to add sound. If you do not have a file to use, open the `bouncing.fla` file from the `Chapter 5` folder. There is also a `bouncing_demo.fla` if you want to see an example of the completed exercise.

How to do it...

1. Make sure the sound is turned on for your computer.

2. Click the new layer button at the bottom left of the timeline to create a new layer named **sound effects** above the layer(s) with graphics drawn on them and below the ActionScript layer if you have one.

3. Create a key frame (*F6*) on the sound effects layer for every point in time in your movie that you want a sound to play. If you are using `bouncing.fla`, create a key frame when the ball hits the bottom of the stage.

4. If the **Sounds** library is not already open, go to **Window | Common Libraries | Sounds**. You can also use your own sound effect by going to **File | Import | Import to Library**.

5. Select a key frame on the sound effect layer that you want to add sound to, and drag an appropriate sound from the library onto the stage. Repeat this for each of the key frames you made that should have sound added to them.

6. Save the file (*Ctrl/Cmd S*), and test the movie (*Ctrl/Cmd Return*). While testing the movie, you should hear the sound effect(s) you added.

How it works...

This timeline in Flash is similar to the user-based button timeline in which the user must do something (like rollover the button) to activate a response. The difference is that the sound effect will play when the movie reaches a specific point in the timeline instead of waiting for the user to perform a specific action. The movie accesses the sound file in the **Library** and plays it at the appropriate time.

See also

▶ *Adding sound effects to a button*

Streaming sound and coding a simple On/Off music button

For longer elements of sound, like a song, it is a good idea to stream the sound rather than embed it into the Flash movie. This helps to keep your file size and load time down. It also gives you more control over starting and stopping the sound. So, if you want to include a song or a longer element of music/sound in your SWF, stream the sound.

Also, if you are planning to have music/lengthy sound files as part of your blog, it is polite and savvy to give viewers the option of turning the sound off. They may prefer their own music as a soundtrack to your blog. They may also be viewing your blog in a professional or other setting where sound is not appropriate.

Getting ready

Make sure that you have sound files (MP3 and WAV files are great) saved in the same location in which you are going to save your SWF file. There is a sound file in the Chapter 5 folder. You can also download songs, loops, and sound effects from a number of different websites such as www.flashkit.com and www.creativecommons.org.

How to do it...

1. In Flash, create a new file by going to **File | New** (*Cmd/Ctrl N*). Select **Flash File (ActionScript 3.0),** and hit **OK**.

2. Go to **Insert | New Symbol**. Name the symbol **mc_stopPlay**. Choose **Movie Clip,** and click **OK.**

3. *Double click* on the symbol in the **Library** to isolate it and view its timeline.

4. Rename the layer buttons.

5. On the first key frame of the buttons layer, place or create a stop button. Go to **Window | Common Libraries | Buttons** to find pre-made buttons if you need. In the Properties panel, name this symbol instance **stop_btn.**

6. Select the second frame in the **buttons** layer, and create a new blank key frame (*F7*).

7. On the second key frame of the buttons layer, place or create a play button. In the Properties panel, name this symbol instance **play_btn.**

8. Create a new layer by clicking the new layer button at the bottom left of the timeline. Name this layer **actions.**

9. Select the first key frame of the **actions** layer, and go to **Window | Actions.**

10. Put the following code into the **Actions** panel with the name of your sound file in place of `song.mp3`:

```
this.stop();

var audio:Sound = new Sound(new URLRequest("song.mp3"));

audio.play();

stop_btn.addEventListener(MouseEvent.CLICK, stopAudio);

function stopAudio(event:MouseEvent):void {
flash.media.SoundMixer.stopAll();
gotoAndStop(2);
}
```

11. Select the second frame of the **actions** layer, and create a new blank key frame (*F7*).

12. In the **Actions** panel, type the following code:

```
play_btn.addEventListener(MouseEvent.CLICK, playAudio);

function playAudio(event:MouseEvent):void {
    gotoAndStop(1);
}
```

13. Save the file (*Ctrl/Cmd S*), and test the movie (*Ctrl/Cmd Return*). While testing the movie, you should hear the sound file you named in your code. If you do not, make sure that you have no typos and that the path you used is correct. For instance, if the sound file is in a folder called `songs`, you would type `"songs/mysong.mp3"` instead of just the file name alone.

How it works...

The file is coded so that the sound file should exist externally.

Inside the movie clip on frame 1, the code first tells the Flash player to stop right away inside of this timeline: `this.stop();`

Then, there is a line of code that sets up the variable and class that allow the sound to stream/play while also naming and pointing to the sound file to be used.

`audio.play();` makes the sound file play right away. No button pressing is necessary to make the sound stream initially.

The rest of the code exists to make the `stop_btn` do its job. It, basically, translates into the following: "When `stop_btn` is clicked, stop all sounds and go to and stop on frame 2 of this timeline." Going to and stopping on frame 2 allows you to see the other button and utilize the ActionScript that allows you to stream/play the sound file again.

Frame 2's code is a little less involved. All it has to do is make the `play_btn` send you back to frame 1 where all the coding is already written to get the music to play.

See also

- ▸ *Using buttons in the Common Library*
- ▸ *Designing your own button*
- ▸ *Designing your own stylish MP3 Player*
- ▸ *Coding your own stylish MP3 Player*

Designing your own stylish MP3 player

This technical recipe gives you a method for designing a stylish MP3 player. Everyone's sense of style is different. The overall goal with this is to keep it unobtrusive and sleek while still looking cool. Depending on the amount of time and your skill level, you can absolutely make a simpler version or something much more involved. There are people who spend their entire corporate workday creating gradients on top of gradients next to gradients to make buttons and player applications of all kinds look as shiny, sleek, and realistic as possible. Here, you will learn a little trick and use just two gradients. This design also incorporates a dynamic text field that is optional. The design dimensions can be changed to eliminate the text field if it is unnecessary. The basic design is shown below. The text field, if you choose to incorporate it, will be centered inside the player.

How to do it...

1. In Flash, create a new file by going to **File | New** (*Ctrl/Cmd N*). Select Flash **File (ActionScript 3.0),** and hit **OK**.

2. Go to **Modify | Document** (*Ctrl/Cmd J*), and change the **Dimensions** to **350 px x 120 px**. Change the **Background color** to black, like the following example:

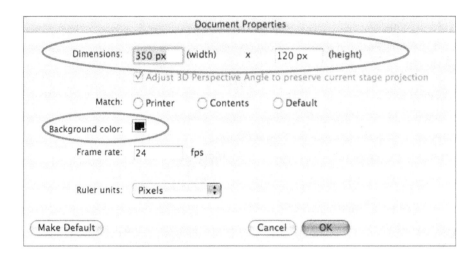

3. Rename **layer 1** to **base panel**.

4. Use the Rectangle Primitive tool to create a rectangle that is 318 x 90 px.

5. In the **Properties** panel, under **Rectangle Options**, round the corners as much as possible. The demo is approximately **39** for each corner.

6. Center align the shape to the stage. Go to **Window > Align**. Click the To Stage button. Click the buttons to center align vertically and horizontally.

7. In the **Color** panel, apply no stroke and a black and white radial gradient for the fill. Then, adjust the gradient so that the white color stop is light grey. Click on the white color stop, and input **#8C8C8C** in the hexadecimal code text field. Use the Gradient Transform tool to alter the gradient like so:

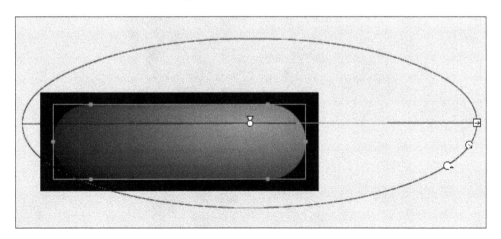

8. With the shape still selected, go to **Edit | Copy** (*Ctrl/Cmd C*).

9. Now, lock this layer.

10. Make a new layer in the timeline by clicking on the new layer button at the bottom left of the panel. Name this layer **top panel**.

11. Go to **Edit | Paste in Place** to make an exact copy of the panel in the exact same location.

12. In the color panel, change the light grey color stop on the gradient bar to white: **#FFFFFF**.

13. With the shape still selected, convert it into a symbol so that a blending mode can be applied. **Modify | Convert to Symbol** (*F8*).

14. **Name** it **mc_sheen,** and for **Type** choose **Movie clip**. Hit **OK.**.

15. In the **Properties** panel, under **Display**, change **Blending** to **Multiply**.

 At any point, you can *double click* on the symbol instance and adjust the position and/or color the gradient to better suit your style needs.

16. Lock this layer.

17. Create a new layer called **text box,** and position it between **base panel** and **top panel** in the timeline layer hierarchy.

18. Grab the Type tool, and create a text box that is **160 x 56 px**. In the **Properties** panel, under **Character**, change the font to **Bauhaus**. If you do not have that font, choose a different font. Set the **Size** to **14.0 pt** and the **Color** to white **#FFFFFF**. At the top of the panel, name this **songDetails,** and change it to **Dynamic Text**, as we see in the example below:

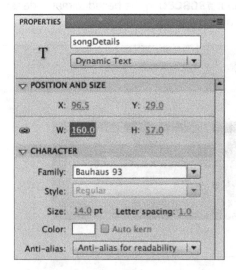

19. Also, under **Paragraph**, make sure that Behavior is **multi-line**. Center align your text.

20. Type a few lines into the text field to see the effect of the top panel on the type. Save the file first, and then test it (*Ctrl/Cmd Return*).

21. Lock this layer for now.

22. Create a new layer at the top of the timeline, and name it **buttons**.

23. Use Flash's type and drawing tools on this layer to create elements that will be converted into buttons. A boomerang shape created by clicking at desired corner points was created for the previous and next buttons. The play and pause buttons are text with these settings:

    ❑ Bauhaus

    ❑ White **#FFFFFF**

    ❑ 12 pts

    ❑ **Letter Spacing**: **1.0**.

24. The previous and pause buttons are positioned on the left side of the player. The next and play buttons are positioned on the right side of the player. This is to make the player look symmetrical. All the buttons are centered vertically to the stage.

25. Select the previous button, and go to **Modify | Convert to Symbol** (*F8*). **Name** it **b_prev**, and for **Type** choose **Button**. Hit **OK**. In the **Properties** panel, name the instance **prev_btn**. *Double click* on the instance. For a bare minimum, give this a **Hit** state. Select the frame for **Hit**, and press *F6* to create a new key frame. Create a rectangle that is slightly larger than the graphic. If you want **Over** and/or **Down** states, create key frames for those states, and alter the graphic or add another element to it. The demo is minimal.

26. Select the next button, and go to **Modify | Convert to Symbol** (*F8*). Name it **b_next**, and for **Type** choose **Button**. Hit **OK**. In the **Properties** panel, name the instance **next_btn**. *Double click* on the instance. Make this button's states match the look and sizing of b_previous. All buttons should have the same look for each state—and a good-sized **Hit** state.

27. Select the pause button, and go to **Modify | Convert to Symbol** (*F8*). **Name** it **b_pause**, and for **Type** choose **Button**. Hit **OK**. In the **Properties** panel, name the instance **pause_btn**. *Double click* on the instance. Make this button's states match the look and sizing of b_previous. All buttons should have the same look for each state—and good-sized **Hit** state.

28. Select the play button, and go to **Modify | Convert to Symbol** (*F8*). **Name** it **b_play**, and for **Type** choose **Button**. Hit **OK**. In the **Properties** panel, name the instance **play_btn**. *Double click* on the instance. Make this button's states match the look and sizing of b_previous. All buttons should have the same look for each state—and good-sized **Hit** state.

29. Select each button in turn, and adjust the transparency of each to different settings so that the shading change seems to affect them also. Go to the **Properties** panel: **Color Effects: Style: Alpha** to do this. The demo uses the following settings:

    ❑ prev_btn: 24%

    ❑ pause_btn: 34%

    ❑ play_btn: 54%

    ❑ next_btn: 38%

30. Unlock the **text box** layer, and line it up vertically as best you can so that the baseline of the middle line of text lines up with the baseline for the play and pause buttons. You can go to **View | Rulers** and drag a guide down from inside the top ruler to help you in your efforts.

31. Save!

How it works...

Flash has a fair number of drawing tools to help you in your efforts as a designer of cool Flash apps and animations. Applying gradients over the top of one another and changing the blending modes and/or transparency settings on the top elements helps to make your design look more complex and dimensional. In order to apply a blending mode or transparency setting, you must have an element of text, a movie clip, or a button. Transparency and blending modes apply to the element they are placed on and allow the look of that element to be affected by the color and tints/shades of the elements below it. The elements on top will not be affected by the transparency and blending mode changes.

This means that the blending mode change on the **top panel** layer only affects the **text box** and the **base panel** layers. The **buttons** layer must be above the **top panel** layer in the timeline so that you can still click on the buttons! To compensate for the loss of the gradient's effect, you change the transparency of each button to a different setting to give the illusion of its being affected by the shade shift.

See also

▶ *Designing your own button*

▶ *Creating a complex button*

Coding your own stylish MP3 player

You have designed a player that is intended to play multiple MP3 (or other) sound files. The player has buttons to go to the next song, the previous song, pause a song, and continue playing a song. Now, you need code. This is the recipe for that code.

Getting ready

Have a Flash file that has previous, next, pause, and play buttons. Name them as follows so that you can directly copy the code in this recipe:

- previous: prev_btn
- next: next_btn
- play: play_btn
- pause: pause_btn

If you do not have a file prepped, use the `player.fla` file in the `Chapter 5` folder. Delete the dynamic text field if you are not planning on using it. Coding for the dynamic text field is not covered in the body of this recipe but in the *There's more* section of *Displaying song information on your MP3 player*.

Also, have more than one sound/music file available to you and saved in the same folder/location that you are saving the `FLA` and `SWF` for this recipe.

If you want to see the demo working, take a look at `player_coded.fla` in the `Chapter 5` folder.

How to do it...

1. Make sure that the buttons in your design really are named as follows:
   - previous: prev_btn
   - next: next_btn
   - play: play_btn
   - pause: pause_btn

2. Make a new layer at the top of the timeline by clicking the new layer button at the bottom left of the timeline, and name it **actions**.

3. Go to **Window | Actions**, and put the following code into the text area (change the names of the MP3 files to match your file names):

```
var playList:Array = new Array("song.mp3", "song1.mp3", "song2.
mp3", "song3.mp3");
var nowPlaying:Boolean = false;
```

```actionscript
var currentSong:Number = 0;
var song:Sound;
var channel:SoundChannel = new SoundChannel();
var position:int;

loadSong(playList[currentSong]);

function playSong(position:Number):void {
    if (!nowPlaying) {
        nowPlaying = true;
        channel = song.play(position);
        channel.addEventListener(Event.SOUND_COMPLETE, songEnded);
    }
}

function pauseSong():void {
    position=channel.position;
    channel.stop();
    nowPlaying = false;
}

function nextSong():void {
    if (currentSong < playList.length - 1) {
        currentSong++;
        pauseSong();
        loadSong(playList[currentSong]);
    }
}

function prevSong():void {
    if (currentSong > 0) {
        currentSong--;
        pauseSong();
        loadSong(playList[currentSong]);
    }
}

function playNow(event:MouseEvent):void {
    playSong(channel.position);
}

function pauseHere(event:MouseEvent):void {
    pauseSong();
}

function goForward(event:MouseEvent):void {
```

```
        nextSong();
    }

    function goBack(event:MouseEvent):void {
        prevSong();
    }

    function loadSong(thisSong:String):void {
        song = new Sound();
        song.load(new URLRequest(thisSong));
        playSong(0);
    }

    function songEnded(event:Event):void {
        pauseSong();
        nextSong();
    }
    play_btn.addEventListener(MouseEvent.CLICK, playNow);
    pause_btn.addEventListener(MouseEvent.CLICK, pauseHere);
    next_btn.addEventListener(MouseEvent.CLICK, goForward);
    prev_btn.addEventListener(MouseEvent.CLICK, goBack);
```

4. Save and test (*Ctrl/Cmd Return*). Presto!

How it works...

The code is set up to work with buttons that exist in your Flash document with the names specified in the code. Those names can always be changed as you need. Just make sure the name of the button instance matches what it is called in the code.

First off, variables, classes, and an array are set up. The array is the list of the song file names that are to be played in the order they are to be played. These file names need to match the names of your song files. The other variables/classes are there so that the sound files will stream and the play and pause buttons will work appropriately—pausing the song halfway through and resuming at the same position in the song.

Then, we have a list of functions that work together to move to the next song (and pause/stop the current song so only one is heard at a time), move to the previous song, pause the song, and play the song from the paused position. There are also functions regarding loading a song from the array and what to do when a song has ended.

At the end, there is the list of click events that the Flash player is listening for that will initiate the different functions of the code.

As long as there are no typos and the sound files are in the same folder as the SWF, the player should work just fine.

There's more...

If you would also like to display information about the song, continue to the following section. It adds a few lines to the code in the body of this recipe and is designed for use with a dynamic text field named `songDetails` and the id3 information that is embedded in many (possibly most) MP3 files. Id3 information is metadata and includes items such as track and artist names. So, rather than taking the time to type all of this out yourself and code a whole second array, just use the information that is already embedded in the MP3.

The settings you used for the Character and Paragraph settings in the Properties panel in Flash for the dynamic text box will apply to the id3 information that is displayed in the text box.

To see a demo, take a look at `player_song_details.fla` in the `Chapter 5` folder.

Displaying song information on your MP3 player

1. Make sure that your Flash file has a dynamic text field named `songDetails`.

2. Add the following code to the code from the body of this recipe section:

```
function displayID3(event:Event):void {
    songDetails.text = " '" + song.id3.songName + "' by " + song.
id3.artist;
}
```

3. To change the text that appears inside the dynamic text field with your id3 information, alter the text that is inside the double quotes that are shown above. For instance, make the dynamic text field read the following:
'Song Title' performed by Artist Name.

4. To accomplish this, change `" ' by "` in the code to `" 'performed by "` and, add the following line into the `loadSong` function:

```
song.addEventListener(Event.ID3, displayID3);
```

The completed code for this entire recipe section should look like this (with your own sound file names in place of the examples given):

```
var playList:Array = new Array("song.mp3", "song1.mp3", "song2.mp3",
"song3.mp3");
var nowPlaying:Boolean = false;
var currentSong:Number = 0;
var song:Sound;
var channel:SoundChannel = new SoundChannel();
var position:int;

loadSong(playList[currentSong]);

function playSong(position:Number):void {
    if (!nowPlaying) {
        nowPlaying = true;
```

```
        channel = song.play(position);
        channel.addEventListener(Event.SOUND_COMPLETE, songEnded);
    }
}

function pauseSong():void {
    position=channel.position;
    channel.stop();
    nowPlaying = false;
}

function nextSong():void {
    if (currentSong < playList.length - 1) {
        currentSong++;
        pauseSong();
        loadSong(playList[currentSong]);
    }
}

function prevSong():void {
    if (currentSong > 0) {
        currentSong--;
        pauseSong();
        loadSong(playList[currentSong]);
    }
}

function playNow(event:MouseEvent):void {
    playSong(channel.position);
}

function pauseHere(event:MouseEvent):void {
    pauseSong();
}

function goForward(event:MouseEvent):void {
    nextSong();
}

function goBack(event:MouseEvent):void {
    prevSong();
}

function displayID3(event:Event):void {
    songDetails.text = " '" + song.id3.songName + "' by " + song.id3.
artist;
}

function loadSong(thisSong:String):void {
    song = new Sound();
```

```
        song.load(new URLRequest(thisSong));
        song.addEventListener(Event.ID3, displayID3);
        playSong(0);
    }

    function songEnded(event:Event):void {
        pauseSong();
        nextSong();
    }

    play_btn.addEventListener(MouseEvent.CLICK, playNow);
    pause_btn.addEventListener(MouseEvent.CLICK, pauseHere);
    next_btn.addEventListener(MouseEvent.CLICK, goForward);
    prev_btn.addEventListener(MouseEvent.CLICK, goBack);
```

According to the ActionScript 3.0 Language and Components Reference, there are a number of properties in ActionScript for utilizing id3 information. They are `album`, `artist`, `comment`, `genre`, `songName`, `track`, and `year`. You only use `songName` and `artist` in this recipe.

See also

▶ *Designing your own button*

▶ *Designing your own stylish MP3 player*

▶ *Coding a simple on/off music button*

6
Flash Applications

In this chapter, we will cover the following:

- ▸ WP-Cumulus plugin 1.22
- ▸ Tagnetic Poetry plugin 1.0
- ▸ Flexi Quote Rotator plugin 0.1.3
- ▸ Create a Custom Quote Rotator using XML
- ▸ WP sIFR plugin 0.6.8.1
- ▸ XML Google Maps plugin 1.12.1
- ▸ Integrating Google Maps into your Flash document
- ▸ Datafeedr Random Ads plugin 2.0
- ▸ WP Flash Feed Scroll Reader plugin 1.1.0.0

Introduction

Many WordPress plugins use Flash to add interactive and dynamic elements and features to your site. In this chapter, we will explore a broad range of applications—unique ways to display your tags, how to use fonts outside of the limited set of web only fonts, quote rotators, ad management, scrolling RSS feed displays, and more.

WP-Cumulus (Version 1.22)

We will look at the working of WordPress Cumulus plugin under this recipe.

Getting ready

Tagging your content is easy and advisable. WordPress tags have at least two functions. First, they are a flexible navigational tool, allowing users to see similar posts from a variety of categories. Second, tags are a SEO tool to increase your keyword density. Tags, in their most simple form, are a list of links displayed for individual posts. The tag cloud is a more complex visual representation that outputs all your tags, with larger font sizes to denote tags that are used most frequently. WP-Cumulus is a plugin that creates a 3D rotating tag cloud as a Flash animation. Flash and HTML are used, so you get both visual appeal and SEO utility.

WP-Cumulus is authored by Roy Tanck. The plugin homepage is: `http://www.wordpress.org/extend/plugins/wp-cumulus/`

WP-Cumulus requires WordPress version 2.3 or newer.

How to do it...

1. Download and install the plugin by going to **Plugins | Add New** and search for "WP-Cumulus."

2. Click **Install** and **Activate**.

3. Visit the plugin configuration page by clicking on **Settings | WP Cumulus**.

4. Choose your **Display Options** for **Width**, **Height**, **Tag Color**, **Background Color**, **Transparency**, and **Speed**. 300px is a good starting width—suggested speeds are 25 to 500. Colors are in hexadecimal format, without the pound sign(#).

5. Choose whether to output tags, categories, or both.

6. Click **Update Options**.

7. There are three ways to insert the tag cloud:

   ❑ To insert the tag cloud into a page or a post, use the following shortcode: `[wp-cumulus]`

   ❑ To insert the tag cloud anywhere in your template files, use the following PHP code: `<?php wp_cumulus_insert(); ?>`

   ❑ To insert the tag cloud into your widgetized sidebar, use the WP-Cumulus widget. Note that all of the display and output options are available in the Widget menu—you can have multiple tag clouds with different appearances, if desired.

Note the tag cloud circled in the following image:

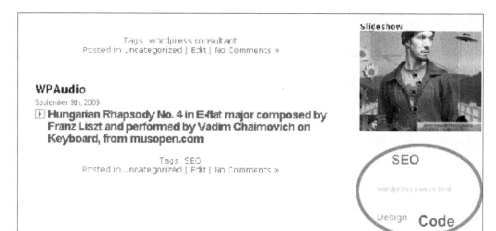

How it works...

WP-Cumulus uses the `wp_tag_cloud` template tag. To change the size of the tags, the maximum number of tags, the order of the tags, or to exclude certain tags, see the Advanced Options on the plugin configuration page (**Settings | WP Cumulus).** These parameters are also available in the WP-Cumulus sidebar widget.

For the complete list of arguments, see the WordPress Codex:

```
http://codex.wordpress.org/Template_Tags/wp_tag_cloud#Parameters
```

There's more...

If you'd like to make changes to the Flash file, Roy is kind enough to provide the source files (released under GNU General Public License) here:

```
http://www.wordpress.org/extend/plugins/wp-cumulus/download/
```

He also shows you how to modify the `.fla` file which allows you to change the font or use different character sets for different languages. See the author's homepage for more information:

```
http://www.roytanck.com/2008/08/04/how-to-add-more-characters-to-wp-
cumulus/
```

Accessing and editing the source files

Go to `http://www.wordpress.org/extend/plugins/wp-cumulus/download/`

In the **Other Versions** section, click on **Development Version** to download the source files. You will get a folder called **wp-cumulus**. Open that folder and then open the **flash sources** folder. There are a number of files inside:

- `com` – This is a folder that holds two ActionScript files inside of other folders.
- `tagcloud_as3.flp` – This is a Flash Project file that can be opened and utilized in the Projects panel in Flash (go to **Window | Other Panels | Projects** to open the panel.) It is a method of keeping multiple files associated with a `FLA` organized and easy to open. It is not mandatory or necessary in this case to use the project file. It's like a bonus feature.
- `tagcloud.fla` – This is the master Flash authoring document. It contains a dynamic text field and a movie clip that is the same size as the stage.
- `tagcloud.swf` – This is the compressed movie.
- `tagcloud.xml` – This is the `XML` file that holds the list of all of the tags to be displayed in the tag cloud.

To change how the tags in the cloud look (or the tag cloud in general), open the `TagCloud.as` file and adjust the ActionScript as desired. For instance, if you want to change the basic color of the tags, change the hexadecimal numbers in the following lines of code:

```
tcolor = ( this.loaderInfo.parameters.tcolor == null ) ? 0x333333
: Number(this.loaderInfo.parameters.tcolor);

tcolor2 = ( this.loaderInfo.parameters.tcolor2 == null ) ? 0x995500
: Number(this.loaderInfo.parameters.tcolor2);

hicolor = ( this.loaderInfo.parameters.hicolor == null ) ? 0x000000
: Number(this.loaderInfo.parameters.hicolor);
```

- `tcolor` is the basic text color when the normal-sized tag is farther back (333333)
- `tcolor2` is the color of the normal sized tag when it is in the front (995500)
- `hicolor` is the highlight color for normal sized tags (000000)

When the tags are larger (due to popularity), then the color change is determined by these lines of code:

```
private function getColorFromGradient( perc:Number ):Number {
        var r:Number = ( perc * ( tcolor >> 16 ) ) + ( (1-perc) * (
tcolor2 >> 16 ) );

    var g:Number = ( perc * ( (tcolor >> 8) % 256 ) ) + ( (1-perc) * (
(tcolor2 >> 8) % 256 ) );
```

```
    var b:Number = ( perc * ( tcolor % 256 ) ) + ( (1-perc) * ( tcolor2
% 256 ) );
    return( (r << 16) | (g << 8) | b );
```

The color numbers here are based on RGB values from 0 to 256. The color is being applied based on the percent (perc) determined earlier in the code.

To adjust the setting for the tags, rather than for the entire cloud, make changes to the Tag.as file. Here, you find code elements for font, mouse events, and more.

There are many more facets of the code that can be altered. Above is a baseline example. Also, inside the ActionScript files, Roy Tanck does a great job of adding comments to his code to explain the purposes of different sections.

In addition to changing the ActionScript files, you can also add and delete information from the XML file as well. For example, you can change links and add tags.

See also

▸   *Tagnetic Poetry plugin (Version 1.0)*

Tagnetic Poetry plugin (Version 1.0)

Tagnetic Poetry is another plugin using Flash to display your blog's tag cloud.

Getting ready

For another take on tags, we'll now explore the Tagnetic Poetry plugin version 1.0 by Roy Tanck & Merel Zwart. Many people are familiar with magnetic poetry sets—a collection of thin magnetized words that you can arrange (and rearrange) to make your own poetry. This plugin uses Flash to display your tags (and categories) in a similar manner. Tags are converted to graphics, which users can arrange and rearrange. Hence the name, Tagnetic Poetry. Clicking on a tag takes the user to a list of all posts tagged with that word. Similar to WP-Cumulus, this plugin uses HTML and Flash so can be considered both user and SEO friendly.

How to do it...

1. Download and install the plugin by going to **Plugins | Add New** and search for "Tagnetic."

2. Click **Install** and **Activate**.

3. Visit the plugin configuration page by clicking on **Settings | Tagnetic Poetry**.

4. Choose your **Tagnetic Poetry Options** for **Width, Height, Size, Background Color,** and **Transparency**.

5. Choose whether to output tags, categories, or both.

6. Click **Update Options**.

7. To insert the tag cloud into a page or a post, use the following shortcode: `[tagneticpoetry]` (You can use parameters in the shortcode, such as `[tagneticpoetry args="number=3"]` to show three tags.)

8. To insert the tag cloud anywhere in your template files, use the following PHP code: `<?php tagneticpoetry_insert(); ?>`

9. To insert the tag cloud into your widgetized sidebar, use the Tagnetic Poetry widget. Note that all of the display and output options are available in the Widget menu—you can have multiple tag clouds with different appearances, if desired.

    Note the Tagnetic Poetry widget in the following image:

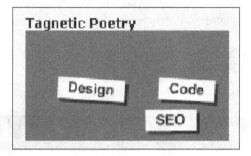

There's more...

If you'd like to make changes to the Flash file, the source files are released under GNU General Public License.

Accessing the Flash source files

To make changes to the Flash file itself, use the source files located here: `http://svn.wp-plugins.org/tagnetic-poetry/`

1. When you get to this page, you are faced with bulleted links:
    - **branches/**
    - **tags/**
    - **trunk/**

2. Click on `trunk/`.

3. Click on `flash_sources/`. This gives you access to a number of source files, including the `FLA`.

4. *Right click/Control click* on `tagcloud.fla` and select **Download Linked File to Desktop** (or a similar choice) to download the Flash file.

5. Click on **com/** and follow the tree through **roytanck/** and **tagneticpoetry/** to get to the ActionScript files. It is these files that you will need to access and alter in order to change the functionality and look of the tag displayer.

6. *Right click/Control click* on **Tag.as** and select **Download Linked File to Desktop** (or a similar choice) to download that file. It primarily allows you to change the look of the individual tags and what change happens upon a mouse event.

7. *Right click/Control click* on **TagCloud.as** and select **Download Linked File to Desktop** (or a similar choice) to download that file. This code deals with the look and functionality of the tag cloud as a whole.

[To simply view the files without downloading them, just click on the links.]

See also

▶ *WP-Cumulus*

▶ *WP-Cumulus: Accessing and editing the source files*

Flexi Quote Rotator plugin (Version 0.1.3)

The following section describes the Flexi Quote Rotator plugin.

Getting ready...

The Flexi Quote Rotator (version 0.1.3) allows you to display a rotating list of quotes on your blog. It uses Flash to create the animation, including a customizable fade out transition between quotes. Insertion is easy—using a widget, shortcode, or PHP. Flexi Quote Rotator is authored by Aidan Curran, using the Quote Rotator plugin by Luke Howell. The plugin homepage is `http://sww.co.nz/wordpress-plugins/flexi-quote-rotator/`.

How to do it...

1. Download and install the plugin by going to **Plugins** | **Add New** and search for "Flexi Quote."

2. Click **Install** and **Activate**.

3. The first step is to enter your list of quotes. To do so, visit **Tools** | **Quotes**:

You can use HTML in either the quote or quote author field.

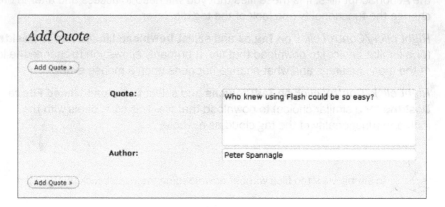

Add Quote

Add Quote »

Quote: Who knew using Flash could be so easy?

Author: Peter Spannagle

Add Quote »

4. Once the quotes are added, they appear for easy editing:

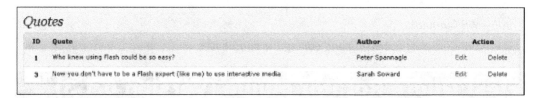

Quotes

ID	Quote	Author	Action	
1	Who knew using Flash could be so easy?	Peter Spannagle	Edit	Delete
3	Now you don't have to be a Flash expert (like me) to use interactive media	Sarah Soward	Edit	Delete

5. To insert the quote rotator into a page or a post, use the following shortcode: `[quoteRotator]`

6. You can optionally use parameters in the shortcode to specify the title, as well as the delay and fade transition time in seconds: `[quoteRotator title="My Title" delay="6" fade="3"]`

7. To insert the quote rotator anywhere in your template files, use the following PHP code: `<?php echo $quoteRotator->getQuoteCode(); ?>`

8. Pass parameters using the following syntax: `<?php echo $quoteRotator->getQuoteCode("My Title", 6, 3); ?>`

9. To insert the tag cloud into your widgetized sidebar, use the **Quote: Flexi Quote Rotator** widget and choose your display options.

The plugin is not designed to display more than one quote area per page.

10. Visit **Settings | Quote Rotator** to choose from five built-in CSS stylesheet options.

Flexi Quote Rotator Options

Title

(adds a header above quote area, leave blank if no header desired)

Delay (in seconds)

Fade duration (in seconds)

Random?   Yes ○   No ◉

Stylesheet   narrow-rounded.css ▼

(you can add your own stylesheet to the directory /wp-content/plugins

Save Changes

Note the Flexi Quote Rotator in the following image:

Flexi Quote Rotator
Now you don't have to be a
Flash expert (like me) to use
interactive media
                    Sarah Soward

There's more...

Perhaps you would like to adjust the styling used to create your quotes. There are two ways to do this—using Photoshop or using CSS. Aidan includes the `.psd` documents that make up the background images. These are located in the following directory:
`/wp-content/plugins/flexi-quote-rotator/photoshop-templates`.

Simply connect to your site via FTP and download the `.psd` file, such as
`narrow-rounded.psd`.

Open the file in Photoshop and make your changes. As an example, seen below, we context click the layer, choose **Blending Options** and select the **Stroke** menu. Set the position to **Inside** and the **Fill Type** to **Gradient** to create a nice effect.

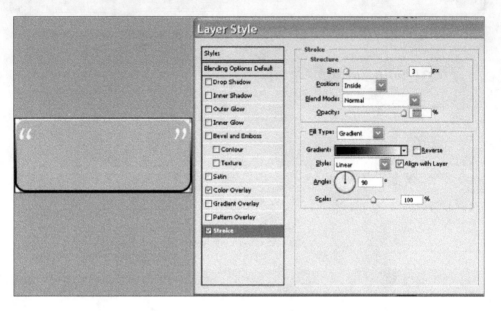

Be sure to export the final image as a `.gif` and overwrite the existing `narrow-rounded.gif` file in the `wp-content/plugins/flexi-quote-rotator/styles/images` directory.

To adjust the CSS, navigate to the following directory:
`/wp-content/plugins/flexi-quote-rotator/styles/`

Here, you will find the four stylesheets included with the plugin, as well as the `/images` directory that contains the images used. You can download the file to edit, such as `narrow-rounded.css`.

Here, we add the color property to make the font an orange color:

```
#quoterotator {
    line-height: 135%;
    color: #e17d49;
}
```

We will also need to make an adjustment to the height to accommodate the 3px border added to all sides—increasing the value from 100px to 106px:

```
#quotearea {
    background: url(images/narrow-rounded.gif) center  no-repeat;
    width: 230px;
    height: 106px;
    padding: 12px 35px 0 35px;
    margin: 15px auto;
}
```

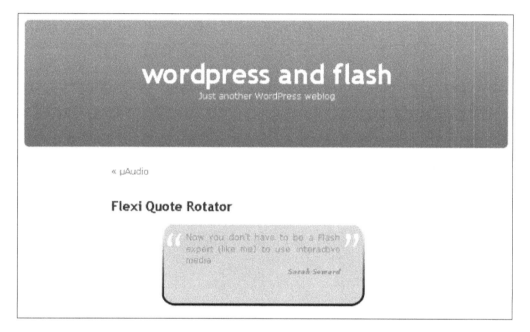

See also

 ▸ *Creating a custom Quote Rotator using XML*

Creating a custom Quote Rotator using XML

If you want to make a Quote Rotator to your own specifications, it is entirely possible do to so with Flash. In this recipe, you will create a custom Quote Rotator. The quotes will be fed into the SWF from an XML file. A wipe effect is used in this recipe. A fade effect is outlined in the *There's more...* section.

Getting ready

If you want to see a demo, it is located in the Chapter 6 folder.

How to do it...

1. Create an XML file using the text editor of your choice.
2. Input the following code:

```
<?xml version="1.0" encoding="UTF-8"?>

<data>

    <quote>There's a special joy that comes with tweening.</quote>

    <quote>See?  You, too, can create SWFs from scratch.</quote>

    <quote>Randomness is good for the soul. </quote>

    <quote>If you code it, they will come.</quote>

    <quote>Movie clips and text fields and code - Oh my!</quote>

    <quote>Ancient proverb: To code a site is to truly know a
site.</quote>

    <quote>Speaking of randomness, how do you feel about ducks?
</quote>

    <quote>Math is fun.  So is Flash.  Put them together and what
do you get?  Well, this.</quote>

</data>
```

3. Type anything you want inside the `<quote> </quote>` tags.
4. Save the file as quotes.xml.
5. In Flash, create a new file by going to **File | New** (*Cmd/Ctrl N*).
6. Select **Flash File (ActionScript 3.0)** and hit **OK**.
7. Go to **File | Save As** and save this file as quote_rotator.fla.
8. Set the stage size and background color to whatever is appropriate for your design and quote length. The demo is #003333, 800px wide and 50px tall. Go to **Modify | Document** (*Ctrl/Cmd J*) to do this.
9. *Double click* on the layer in the timeline and rename it text.
10. Use the Type tool to create a text field that is the size you need for your design. The demo is 750px x 20px.

11. In the **Properties** panel, name the text block `text_txt` and give it attributes such as a font and font size. The demo is set to `Lithos Pro, Regular, 14pt`. The text color is #CCCCCC. Click the **Embed** button to embed the font.

12. Select the text block with the Selection tool and go to **Modify | Convert to Symbol** (*F8*). Name the symbol `mc_quote` and choose **Movie Clip** for **Type**. Hit **OK**.

13. In the **Properties** panel, name this movie clip `quote_mc`.

14. Use the **Align** or **Properties** panel to position the movie clip as necessary. In the demo, the movie clip is centered vertically and horizontally.

15. Create a new layer in the timeline by clicking on the new layer button at the bottom left of the panel. *Double click* on the layer name to rename this layer `actions`.

16. Go to **Window | Actions** (*F9/Option F9*) to pull out the **Actions** panel.

17. Put the following code into the panel:

```
import fl.transitions.*;
import fl.transitions.easing.*;

var quotes:Array = new Array();
var randomNumber:Number;
var textTween:Tween;

var rotateTimer:Timer = new Timer(7000);
rotateTimer.addEventListener("timer",", nextQuote);
rotateTimer.start();

var xml:XML;
var xmlPath:String = "quotes.xml";
var loader:URLLoader = new URLLoader();
var myXML:URLRequest = new URLRequest(xmlPath);
loader.addEventListener(Event.COMPLETE, loadComplete);
loader.load(myXML);

function loadQuotes():void{
    for each(var item:XML in xml.quote){
        quotes.push(item);
    }
}

function randomness():void{
    randomNumber = Math.round(Math.random() * (quotes.length - 1));
    quote_mc.quote_txt.text = quotes[randomNumber];
    TransitionManager.start(quote_mc, {type:Wipe,
direction:Transition.IN, duration:3, easing:Regular.easeOut,
startPoint:1});
}
```

```
function loadComplete(event:Event):void{
    xml = new XML(event.target.data);
    loadQuotes();
    randomness();
}
function nextQuote(event:TimerEvent):void{
    randomness();
}
```

18. Save the file and test it (*Ctrl/Cmd Return*).

How it works...

The quotes are pulled from the `<quote>` tags in the XML document and populate the SWF file. This is done via ActionScript.

The XML file is denoted in the line:

```
var xmlPath:String = "quotes.xml";
```

This path can be changed as needed to point to the location of the XML file you are using.

Making the quotes appear in a random order is primarily handled in the `randomness` function. The quote shown is figured through a little bit of `Math`.

The amount of times a quote shows up is controlled by the number in this line of code:

```
var rotateTimer:Timer = new Timer(7000);
```

The number is a value in milliseconds. The demo has a quote showing up for seven seconds including the time it takes for the wipe in effect.

The wipe in effect is primarily dealt with in this line of code:

```
TransitionManager.start(quote_mc, {type:Wipe, direction:Transition.
IN, duration:3, easing:Regular.easeOut, startPoint:1});
```

The visibility change (`Wipe`, `TransitionIN`) is applied to the movie clip named `quote_mc`. The type of ease used in the demo is `Regular.easeOut`. This means the animation change starts fast and then slows down. This visibility change starts at 1 (representing the top left corner) and proceeds through to wipe in the entire movie clip at end point 9 (representing the bottom right corner of the movie clip). The numbers 1-9 can be visualized as the bounding box points when you select your movie clip with the Free Transform tool. Feel free to test a different `startPoint`.

There's more...

There's more than one way to tween a symbol.

Additional transitions exist. These are `Blinds`, `Fade`, `Fly`, `Iris`, `Photo`, `PixelDissolve`, `Rotate`, `Squeeze`, `Wipe`, and `Zoom`. The transitions have the same properties with the exception of the last, which is specific to the transition chosen. `Fade` requires an `alpha` change, whereas `Wipe` requires a `startPoint`.

There are other easing options available per Adobe. Classes in addition to `Regular` are `Back`, `Bounce`, `Elastic`, `None`, and `Strong`. For the purposes of legibility, `Regular` and `Strong` are your best bets.

To further modify the ease, there are three methods: `easeOut`, `easeIn`, `easeInOut`. `easeOut` starts the tween fast and ends it slow; and `easeIn` does the opposite. To get both a slow start and end, use `easeInOut`, just make sure that you have enough time in your timer for it to render well.

Fading the text in your Rotator

In your Flash file, access your ActionScript in the Actions panel (*F9/Option F9*).

Change this line of code:

```
TransitionManager.start(quote_mc, {type:Wipe, direction:Transition.
IN, duration:3, easing:Regular.easeOut, startPoint:1});
```

to this line of code:

```
TransitionManager.start(quote_mc, {type:Fade, direction:Transition.
IN, duration:3, easing:Regular.easeOut, alpha:0});
```

If you prefer to have the text start out 100% opaque and then fade out, try this line of code instead:

```
TransitionManager.start(quote_mc, {type:Fade, direction:Transition.
OUT, duration:7, easing:Regular.easeIn, alpha:0});
```

This is a simple fade out effect that should be set to the same amount of time as the duration of each quote. If your timer is set to 7,000 milliseconds, then set your duration for the fade out effect to 7 seconds.

See also

▶ *Flexi Quote Rotator plugin 0.1*

WP sIFR (Version 0.6.8.1)

The following section talks about the WP sIFR plugin.

Getting ready...

You are probably aware that web pages use a limited set of fonts. Your word processing program allows you to choose from a wide variety of fonts—as many as are installed on your computer. So why can't you use these fonts on your web page? Since a web page needs to be available to users with many different system configurations, there is no way to be sure which fonts they have installed. The solution has been to use a set of web only fonts that are standard on all systems.

New solutions are in place today to deliver rich typography on the Web, including fonts outside of the standard web-only font families. In this section, we'll explore sIFR, or Scalable Inman Flash Replacement. This new technology uses Flash to recreate and replace text you've tagged to be "sIFRed." WP sIFR allows you to use custom fonts on your WP blog. WP sIFR version 0.6.8.1 is authored by Jake Snyder. The plugin homepage is: `http://labs.jcow.com/plugins/wp-sifr/`

How to do it...

1. Download and install the plugin by going to **Plugins | Add New** and search for "sIFR."

2. Click **Install** and **Activate**.

3. The first step is to convert a True Type Font (`.ttf`) into a sIFR `.swf` file by using the sIFR generator, available here: `http://www.sifrgenerator.com/wizard.html`

4. Browse to your `Fonts` folder to locate the address of a font to use, such as: `C:\WINDOWS\Fonts\BickhamScriptPro-Bold.otf`

5. You can convert an `.otf` file to a `.ttf` file by following the Online Font Converter link in the sidebar: `http://www.onlinefontconverter.com/`

6. Copy and paste the address from the `.ttf` file into the **TrueType Font** field and click **Next**:

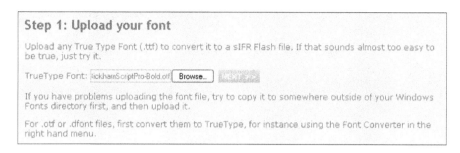

7. Choose the sIFR version to use and click **Next**. You must use the most up to date version—sIFR 3 r436:

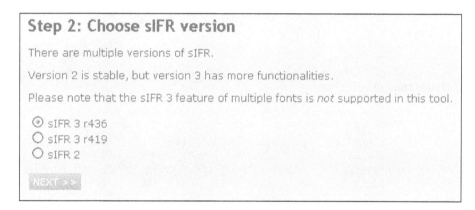

8. Choose which characters you need, based on your intended use, and click **Next**. We choose **Letters, digits and common other characters**:

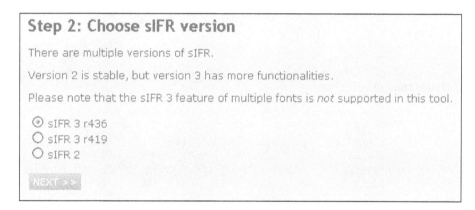

9. Enter the verification word.

10. Review your choices and click **Next**:

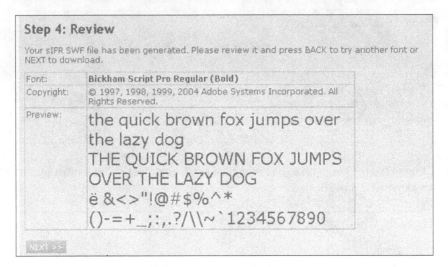

11. **Download** the `.swf` file:

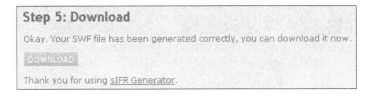

12. Remove any spaces from the file name and upload the `.swf` file to a folder named `fonts` within your theme directory, such as: `/wp-content/themes/default/fonts`

 The plugin looks in two places for font files: a `/fonts` folder in your active theme, or `wp-content/plugins/wp-sifr/fonts`. If you use the `plugin` folder instead of the `theme` folder, your fonts will be deleted when using the WordPress automatic upgrade option for plugins. For this reason, using the `theme` folder is recommended.

13. Visit the plugin configuration page by clicking on **Settings | WP sIFR**.

14. Check the **Activate this font** checkbox to activate the new font:

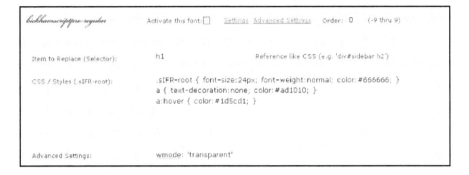

15. The **Item to Replace (Selector)** menu is where you specify which tags to replace. To use more than one selector, simply use commas. Our example is **h1**.

16. Click on **Settings** to set CSS styling. Our example is:

```
.sIFR-root { font-size:64px; font-weight:normal; color:#666666;
text-align: center; width: 708px;}
a { text-decoration:none; color:#ffffff; }
a:hover { color:#ad1010; }
```

Please note that the font-weight property must match your font—bold is only a valid value if you have uploaded the bold version of the font. sIFR will not display unless the font you've uploaded and the font-weight property match.

17. Click on **Advanced Settings** to edit additional Flash variables. The following sets the background color of the Flash animation—either one or the other is required to display correctly in Internet Explorer: wmode: 'transparent' or wmode: 'opaque'.

18. Click **Save Changes**.

How it works...

sIFR utilizes JavaScript, CSS, and Flash to deliver rich typography to your users. Your page loads normally by using HTML or XHTML. Then, JavaScript verifies that Flash is installed and looks for text you've tagged to be replaced. If Flash is not installed or if JavaScript is blocked, the normal page is delivered. Otherwise, the script creates Flash objects that output your text in a new font and replace the elements you've tagged with these animations.

There's more...

Support documentation for this plugin is located at: `http://wiki.novemberborn.net/sifr3/How+to+use#main`. Among other things, the documentation explains the implementation and editing of the discrete parts of the plugin. To see the information pertaining specifically to Flash, click on **Flash Configuration** or **Filters. Flash Configuration** shows you the options to change for the `flash/Options.as` file. The **Filters** page lists the different types of filters and the properties that belong to them. You can edit the filters by simply changing the hexadecimal code for the color of something (e.g. - change #000000 to #CCCCCC) or even add another filter such as a Bevel. Just make sure that you follow the same format shown on `http://wiki.novemberborn.net/sifr3/Filters` to ensure that the code will work:

```
filters: {
  DropShadow: {
    knockout: true
    ,distance: 1
    ,color: '#330000'
    ,strength: 2
}
}
```

 Please note that the Flash coding language used for this plugin is ActionScript 2.0.

More Info

For a Flash-less alternative to rich typography, see FLIR for WordPress: `http://www.wordpress.org/extend/plugins/facelift-image-replacement/`

XML Google Maps plugin (Version 1.12.1)

The following section talks about the XML Google Maps plugin.

Getting ready...

The XML Google Maps plugin, version 1.12.1, by Patrick Matusz, allows easy sharing of custom maps in a variety of formats, including My Google Maps and Google Earth Plugin Maps. With this handy tool, you can also share a map of your geo-tagged Flickr photostream, Picasa Web Album Picture Map, or Next-Gen Gallery album, if your NextGEN Gallery Images are already Geocoded (EXIF). To Geocode your photos, use a free utility such as iTag, available here: `http://itagsoftware.com/`

The English language homepage for the plugin is: `http://www.matusz.ch/blog/projekte/xml-google-maps-wordpress-plugin-en/`

Before getting started, the first step is to create a My Google Map. You will need to sign up for a Google Maps API key here: `http://code.google.com/apis/maps/signup.html`

To add geo tags to your Flickr photos, log in to your Flickr account and click on **Organize | Your Map**.

How to do it...

1. Download and install the plugin by going to **Plugins | Add New** and search for "XML map."

2. Click **Install** and **Activate**.

3. Visit the plugin configuration panel at **Settings | XML Google Maps**.

4. In the Basic Options Menu, enter your Google API key.

5. Also, enter the width for your Map (see Chapter 1, *Edit and debug with Firebug* for an overview of how to use Firebug to inspect your site's CSS). In our example, the width of the `.narrowcolumn` class of the content `<div>` in the default Kubrik theme is 450px.

6. Scroll down to review the additional menus. We suggest you look at the first three menus at least: **Control Options**, **Map Type Options**, and **Map Behaviour Options**. Make choices appropriate to your application. Settings are available for map alignment, pan/zoom, map type (satellite, hybrid, normal, physical, or Google Earth plugin), etc.

7. Click **Save Changes**.

8. To insert a map, create a new page or post. You simply need to make a link to your Google My Map. Click on the **Link** button of your Google My Map and copy the URL. Our example is: `<a href="http://maps.google.com/maps/ms?hl=en&gl=us &ie=UTF8&view=map&vps=1&jsv=178b&msa=0&output=nl&msid=100648506 111875485976.000475b2cc9bbf6187ef6">Packt Publishing</a>`

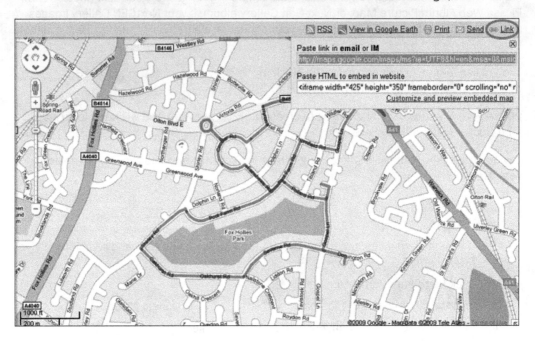

There's more...

Inserting a geo-tagged Flickr stream is just as easy. Patrick provides a nice overview here: `http://www.matusz.ch/blog/projekte/xml-google-maps-wordpress-plugin-en/samples/n10/`

Visit your Flickr homepage and scroll to the bottom of the page. Look for the RSS logo and link; to the right is a KML link. Context-click and copy the link location:

You must edit this link, removing the section that contains `&lang=en-us`:

```
http://api.flickr.com/services/feeds/geo/?id=37640425@N06&lang=en-
us&format=kml_nl
```

becomes:

```
http://api.flickr.com/services/feeds/geo/?id=37640425@N06&format=kml_
nl
```

Then, insert into a page or post using the following format:

```
[xmlgm {http://api.flickr.com/services/feeds/geo/?id=37640425@
N06&format=kml_nl}]
```

Integrating Google Maps into your Flash document

It is possible to incorporate a scrollable map from Google into a SWF. This recipe tells you how to do that. The steps are modified from the very effective tutorial at `http://code.google.com/apis/maps/documentation/flash/intro.html`. This recipe is honed down to the essential steps for working specifically with Flash CS4 and Google Maps API library. A perk of incorporating a Google map in this fashion, rather than just using a static bitmap image of a map, is that as Google updates their map library, you get to reap the benefits of those updates.

Getting ready

You must have a URL that belongs to you in order to get an API key from Google to use their Google Maps API library.

Go to `http://code.google.com/apis/maps/signup.html` to sign up for the Google Maps API. It is not possible to incorporate an interactive Google map into a SWF web page without doing this first. There is a list of requirements as well as terms and conditions that you must agree to and abide by in order to use this. By signing up, you will receive an API key that will be used/referenced in your ActionScript. Each domain name that you want to use a Google Map in will need to have its own API key as the key is specific to your URL. The key will be a long line of numbers and letters.

Have the latitude and longitude of the location you want centered in your map. There are many websites that can provide latitude and longitude. You can use a search engine of your choice to search for such sites.

How to do it...

1. If you have not already done so, go to http://code.google.com/apis/maps/ signup.html to sign up for the Google Maps API.

2. Download the Google Maps API for Flash library from http://code.google.com/ apis/maps/documentation/flash/intro.html. The link is located in the **Obtaining the Interface Library** section. There are two folders in the sdk folder that is downloaded: docs and lib.

3. Navigate to the lib folder and open it to see the two files inside. One is specific to Flash development (map_1_16.swc), the other is specific to use with Adobe Flex Builder (map_flex_1_16.swc). The numbers associated with the files represent the version and may differ from what is shown here. You will use the Flash-oriented file.

4. Make sure that Flash is closed.

5. Create a folder named Google in the following directory:

   □ For Windows: C:\Program Files\Adobe\Adobe Flash CS4\ language\Configuration\Components

   □ For Mac: Macintosh HD/Applications/Adobe Flash CS4/ Common/Configuration/Components

6. Copy the map_1_16.swc file (again, the number may differ, just make sure it does not have the word flex in the filename) into the Google folder that you just made. You will now be able to access the component library in this file inside of Flash.

Now, you can launch Flash:

1. In Flash, create a new file by going to **File | New** (*Ctrl/Cmd N*).

2. Select **Flash File (ActionScript 3.0)** and hit **OK**.

3. Go to **File | Save As** and save this file as map.fla.

4. Go to **Window | Components** and click on **Google**. Drag the **GoogleMapsLibrary** component onto the stage:

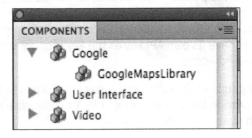

All that will appear on the stage is an empty rectangle with a thin blue line around it to let you know that it is selected. If you deselect the component, nothing of it will be visible. Also, the position of it is not important. ActionScript will be used to control that.

5. Make a new layer at the top of your timeline by clicking on the new layer button at the bottom left of the timeline. Name this layer `actions`.

6. Go to **Window** | **Actions** (*F9/Option F9*) to pull out the **Actions** panel. Make sure the key frame for your actions layer is selected.

7. Place the following code into the **Actions** panel:

```
import com.google.maps.LatLng;
import com.google.maps.Map;
import com.google.maps.MapEvent;
import com.google.maps.MapType;

var map:Map = new Map();
map.key = "your_api_key";
map.setSize(new Point(stage.stageWidth, stage.stageHeight));
map.addEventListener(MapEvent.MAP_READY, onMapReady);
this.addChild(map);

function onMapReady(event:Event):void {
   map.setCenter(new LatLng(37.4419,-122.1419), 14, MapType.NORMAL_
MAP_TYPE);
}
```

 Replace `"your_api_key"` with the actual key from Google. Leave the quotation marks around the key so that the code functions properly.

8. Go to **File** | **Publish Settings** and select the **Flash** tab at the top of the dialog box.

9. Make sure that **Local playback security** is set to **Access network only.** This ensures that the library information will be successfully retrieved from Google. Click **OK**.

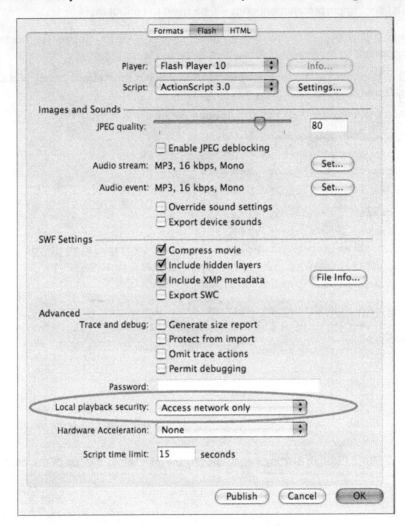

10. Save the file and test the movie.

How it works...

The component that you downloaded from Google allows you to incorporate their map with a modicum of code. It is pre-configured to allow easy usage for you, as with any other component.

The ActionScript used imports four Google Map libraries to call upon in the rest of your code: latitude/longitude, map, map events, and types of maps.

The variable sets up the map class and names it, simply, map.

The map key is set to the key you received from Google when you signed up for the Google Map API. It allows you to access their libraries on your site or blog.

`map.setSize` matches the size of the map to your stage size.

The event listener and handler (the `function`) work together to load the map so that the coordinates you use are at the center of the map when it loads. The zoom level is also set, in this case, at 14. The handler/function also sets the type of map, in this case, a normal map.

`this.addChild(map);` tells the map to load into the root level of the `SWF`.

When the `SWF` is implemented on your site, it will pull map information from the Google Maps API library to display the most updated version of the map that exists in the library. It will display in the fashion that you coded in your ActionScript.

There's more...

Google provides additional information about the different types of maps that can be used, the different zoom levels available, and offers up a way to add informational text. There are still more options at http://code.google.com than are included here.

Types of maps

There are more Map Attributes than just `NORMAL_MAP_TYPE`. There are also:

- `SATELLITE_MAP_TYPE` (Google Earth image)
- `HYBRID_MAP_TYPE` (mixture of `NORMAL` and `SATELLITE`)
- `PHYSICAL_MAP_TYPE` (relief map)
- `DEFAULT_MAP_TYPES` (an array of `NORMAL`, `SATELLITE`, `HYBRID`, and `PHYSICAL`)

Zoom levels

Zoom levels, according to Google, range from 0-19. 0 = the entire world. 19 = individual buildings. With `SATELLITE` view, the zoom level goes to 20.

 Zoom levels are not entirely consistent as different levels of information are available for different parts of the world.

Adding an Information Bubble

According to Google, to add an informative bubble in the center of the map, replace the onMapReady function with the following code in your Flash file:

```
function onMapReady(event:Event):void {
  map.setCenter(new LatLng(37.4419,-122.1419), 14, MapType.NORMAL_MAP_
TYPE);
map.openInFoWindow(getCenter(), new InfoWindowOptions({
    title: "Instructions", "Drag to scroll."
    }));
}
```

See also

▶ *XML Google Maps 1.12.1*

Datafeedr Random Ads V2 (Version 2.0)

The following section talks about the XML Google Maps Datafeedr Random Ads V2 plugin.

Getting ready...

This free plugin allows you to easily insert rotating ads into your theme or sidebar. Just about every type of ad is supported, including Google Adsense, ads from other affiliate programs, banners, flash, images, and text. Version 2 is for use on blogs using WordPress 2.8 or newer. Brought to you by the Datafeedr.com team, the plugin homepage is http://www.datafeedr.com/random-ads-plugin/.

Before getting started, you will want to gather ads to use. A variety of affiliate programs can help get you started. In addition to Google Adsense and Yahoo! Publisher Network, you might consider affiliate programs such as Commission Junction: http://www.cj.com

How to do it...

1. Download and install the plugin by going to **Plugins | Add New** and search for "random ads v2."

2. Click **Install** and **Activate**.

3. Visit the plugin configuration panel at **Tools | Datafeedr Random Ads**.

4. Click on the link to **Add New Group**.

5. Enter an **Ad Group Name**, such as Sidebar.

6. If you want text or HTML before or after your ads, enter it in the **Before Ad** or **After Ad** field, as appropriate.

7. In the first box, **Ad #1**, paste your first ad.

8. Add additional ads by clicking **Add Box**.

To insert a Flash animation, use the full embed code, such as:

```
<object classid="clsid:d27cdb6e-ae6d-11cf-
96b8-444553540000" width="320" height="240"
codebase="http://download.macromedia.
com/pub/shockwave/cabs/flash/swflash.
cab#version=6,0,40,0"><param name="src" value="http://
www.wordpressandflash.com/wp-content/themes/default/
swfobject_test.swf" /><embed type="application/x-
shockwave-flash" width="190" height="143" src="http://
www.wordpressandflash.com/wp-content/themes/default/
swfobject_test.swf"></embed></object>
```

9. When you are finished, click **Save Ad Group**.

10. Click **edit** on your Ad Group to verify that all ads have been entered correctly.

11. The plugin automatically generates code you can insert anywhere in your theme template files. Our example is: `<?php if (function_exists('dfrads')) { echo dfrads('9125849'); } ?>`

    Note the sample ad in the following image:

12. To add the ads to your widgetized sidebar, visit **Appearance | Widgets** and drag and drop the **Datafeedr Random Ads** widget to the appropriate location.

WP Flash Feed Scroll Reader (Version 1.1.0)

The following section talks about the WP Flash Feed Scroll Reader plugin.

Getting ready...

The Flash Feed Scroll Reader allows you to share an RSS feed with your users in a unique format—as a horizontal scrolling Flash animation. Setup and configuration is a snap. Styling is fully customizable, using CSS and XHTML. Version 1.1.0 is authored by Giovambattista Fazioli. The plugin homepage is: http://www.wordpress.org/extend/plugins/flash-feed-scroll-reader/

How to do it...

1. Download and install the plugin by going to **Plugins | Add New** and search for "flash feed."

2. Click **Install** and **Activate**.

3. Visit the plugin configuration panel at **Settings | WP Flash Scroll Feed Reader**.

4. Enter the **Feed URL** to show the feed titles.

5. To show the content of each feed item, check the **Show Feed Item Description** box. Use the **Max chars content** to limit the amount of text displayed.

6. Review the settings for **Width**, **Height**, **Scroll Speed**, etc.

7. If you want to display more than one feed, click the **Use aggregator** box.

8. Click **Save Settings**.

9. The PHP code, a list of arguments, and a convenient preview box all appear below for you: `<?php flashfeedscrollreader() ?>`

10. Copy and paste the code into the appropriate place by visiting **Appearance | Editor** and choosing a template file to modify. In our case, we used the following code: `<div style="margin-left: 10px;"><?php flashfeedscrollreader("wmode=transparent") ?> </div>`

Note the Flash Feed Scroll Reader in the following image:

b Pages in UPK 3.5 *   Exclusive Discount Offer : Drupal 6 Search Engine Optimization - Up to 50% Off

There's more...

Two CSS stylesheets are provided. The default is: `http://www.wordpressandflash.com/wp-content/plugins/flash-feed-scroll-reader/css/style.css`. In the same directory, you will find a `big.css` stylesheet. You can select which stylesheet to use in the plugins configuration page, and make any changes you require to the existing CSS using the same tools and strategies outlined in previous chapters.

7
Flash Themes

In this chapter, we will cover the following:

- ▸ CSS
- ▸ WordPress theme hierarchy
- ▸ WordPress template tags
- ▸ Customizing Kubrik

Introduction

WordPress themes are made up of CSS stylesheets, template files, and template tags. In this chapter, we present an in-depth look at all three. We'll then apply this knowledge by customizing the default Kubrik theme.

Picking a theme—free or premium

Most people new to WordPress start out with a free theme. The advantage is obvious—there is no upfront direct monetary cost. Plus, there are literally thousands of free themes out there to choose from. This can be a good option, depending on your goals. However, if you are serious about your site, we strongly encourage you to consider purchasing a premium theme. The advantages of a premium theme authored by a competent and reputable designer include: expandability, theme documentation and support, cross-browser compatibility, and future upgrades. The costs are reasonable, ranging from $25 to $100.

Whether you pick a free or a premium theme, do yourself a favor and do some research. Make sure it has the functionality you require. Your website's visual identity and core functions will be based on this code, so be sure that you have the right starting point and a solid structure.

What to look for

- A reputable and experienced theme author.

- Extensibility—does the theme design allow for customization? There should be a theme options page, and the design should not rely upon one large background image.

- It uses CSS, instead of tables, for structure.

- It is standards-compliant: valid CSS and XHTML.

- Cross-browser optimized: determine what browsers you will be supporting. Check the site in IE6, IE7, Chrome, Safari, and FireFox. Don't take their word for it—use the following website: `http://www.browsershots.org`

- Support documentation: comprehensive documentation will be helpful as you customize a theme.

CSS

A basic understanding of CSS is essential if you plan on customizing a theme. Each theme has one or more stylesheets—and the name is often `style.css`.

Getting ready

The stylesheet contains many entries that determine how a theme looks. Each entry is called a selector, and each selector has at least one property with a value. All of these rules together create the theme, by specifying all of the structural elements, such as the width of the page and columns, the colors used, fonts, alignment, background images, etc.

How to do it...

CSS syntax is very important. It is always the same, and looks like this:

```
selector {property:value;}
```

Let us emphasize:

1. The properties and values must be wrapped in curly braces.

2. A colon (`:`) must separate a property and a value.

3. A semicolon (`;`) terminates the value, allowing the computer to continue reading.

If you disrupt this syntax, your site will probably not display correctly, or at all.

How it works...

The selector may be one of three types:

- HTML tag
- class
- ID

All of your favorite HTML tags can be styled as a CSS selector. Some examples follow for the common HTML tags body, a `href`, `h1`, and `p`:

```
body {
background-color: white;
padding: 10px;
}

a  {
color: #000000;
}

h1 {
font-size: 24px;
}

p {
font-size 14px;
line-height: 18px;
}
```

Selectors can be grouped by simply using a comma:

```
h1, h2, h3 {
font-color:  #000000;
}

p, body {
line-height: 18px;
}
```

It is very conceivable that your design could require more than one style for HTML tags. Classes allow you to do this. A class starts with a period (.) and can be used as many times as you want:

```
img.centered {
display:block;
margin-left:auto;
margin-right:auto;
}
```

```
img.alignright {
display:inline;
margin:0 0 2px 7px;
padding:4px;
}
img.alignleft {
display:inline;
margin:0 7px 2px 0;
padding:4px;
}
```

To apply a class using XHTML, use the following syntax:

```
should be <img source="http://yourdomain/images/example.jpg"
alt="your
image" class="centered" />
```

Classes do not need to include an HTML tag. Normally, this strategy is used when a class will not be limited to one tag, such as:

```
.alignright {
float:right;
}
```

Another common approach is to use a class with or without an HTML tag when the class will be applied to a `<div>` tag, affecting all of the content found within:

```
.feedback {
    color: #ccc;
    text-align: right;
}
.comments h3{
margin:40px auto 20px;
padding:0;
}
```

Here is an example of a class being applied to a `<div>`. The entire contents (a template tag, which we will explore soon) will be right aligned:

```
<div class="feedback">
    <?php wp_link_pages(); ?>
    <?php comments_popup_link(__('Comments (0)'), __('Comments
(1)'), __('Comments (%)')); ?>
</div>
```

An ID always starts with a pound sign (#). An ID can only be used once per page:

```
#page {
background-color:white;
border:1px solid #959596;
margin:20px auto;
padding:0;
width:760px;
}

#header {
background-color:#73A0C5;
height:200px;
margin:0 0 0 1px;
padding:0;
width:758px;
}

#footer {
margin:0 auto;
padding:0;
width:760px;
}
```

ID's are applied like this:

```
<div id="footer"></div>
```

Block and inline elements

Before proceeding, it is worthwhile to review an important aspect of how HTML works. This will clarify how `<div>` and `<span>` tags are used and why they, and other tags, behave as they do.

HTML can be displayed in one of three ways: block, inline, or hidden. Block elements take up the full width of the space available, with a new line before and after. The `<p>` tag is the most familiar example of a block element. The `<div>` tag is also a block element, as are headings `<h1>`...`<h6>`, unordered lists `<ul>`, and list items `<li>`.

`<div>` tags are simply empty tags, or divisions, that hold other elements and create structure. Think of them like containers. `<div>` is the generic block level tag.

Inline elements get applied without extra spacing. Common inline tags include anchor, bold, italics, image, line break and span: `<a>`, `<b>`, `<i>`, `<img />` `<br />`, and `<span>`. `<span>` is the generic inline tag (a container for inline formatting).

The `<meta />` tag is an example of a hidden element.

As mentioned above, tags have a default setting. So, if you don't declare the display property, the tag will use the its default setting. However, you can easily change how any tag is displayed via CSS. Simply set the display property to one of the three allowed values:

```
display:block;
display:inline;
display:none;
```

Commenting

Comments are incredibly useful. They explain to humans the purpose of code. Also, comments can be used to keep track of revisions. If you are unsure about a change you are going to make to your stylesheet, you can non-destructively edit by placing the piece to be changed inside of a comment.

Comments in CSS may take up more than one line and they start with /* and end with */

Here is an example of non-destructive editing. See how all of the values are changed, but the originals are preserved? A search for CHANGED will quickly take us to the modified parts of the stylesheet:

```
#header {
background-color:#ffffff; /* CHANGED from #73A0C5 */
height:150px; /* CHANGED from 200px */
margin:10px; /* CHANGED from 0 0 0 1px */
padding:5px; /* CHANGED from 0 */
width:858px; /* CHANGED from 758px */
}
```

Template files and theme structure

Once you have an understanding of the CSS basics, getting familiar with the files that make up your theme is the next step.

Getting ready

We've mentioned this before, but it bears repeating that there are no "pages" (in the sense of a single static, tables-based HTML page) in a PHP-driven site like WordPress. All of the data that you add to WordPress (including posts, pages, comments, and users) is added to the MySQL database. The data is filtered through a theme along with the help of plugins to create a website with different pages. But each page is made up of several different pieces. Within a theme, common elements (such as the header, footer, and sidebar) exist as separate PHP template files. These pieces are combined and served based on the theme structure and according to actions taken by a user (such as clicking or searching).

On the front end, your users are able to navigate to (and bookmark) URLs that seem a lot like pages. However, hopefully, you are starting to understand that these URLs, such as the homepage, the category archive view (list of the posts in a given category), or an individual post or page, are in fact a combination of several files. This approach (abandoning static pages and separating content from design) allows you greater flexibility and ease of use. For instance, if you want to, change the header, this is done in one place (one time) and the change occurs automatically and is site wide.

How to do it...

Let's look at `index.php` of the default Kubrik theme to get a better sense of how all this works:

1. Click on **Appearance | Editor**.

2. In the right-hand column below the **Templates** heading, click on **index.php**.

The very first lines call `header.php`:

```php
<?php
/**
 * @package WordPress
 * @subpackage Classic_Theme
 */
get_header();
?>
```

We're going to disregard the comments (a form of file documentation). Simply realize that `<?php get_header(); ?>` inserts the file `header.php`.

Similarly, the file ends with a call to insert the file `footer.php`: `<?php get_footer(); ?>`

These are specific forms of template tags, called include tags. Their purpose, as we have seen, is to provide an easy way to insert the basic template files:

- Header: `<?php get_header(); ?>`
- Sidebar: `<?php get_sidebar(); ?>`
- Comments: `<?php comments_template();?>`
- Footer: `<?php get_footer(); ?>`

To include any template file, use the following:

```php
<?php include( TEMPLATEPATH . '/mytemplate.php' ); ?>
```

This code looks in your theme directory (`wp-content/themes/mytheme`) for a template file of the given name, and inserts it.

For more information, see: `http://codex.wordpress.org/Include_Tags`

How it works...

Now you know how template files are combined within a given file. The next step is to understand which template files are displayed based on user actions. Depending on where a user clicks, different template files will be used. The specifics depend upon your theme structure, but here we present a brief overview of the concept of template hierarchy.

Logic built into WordPress evaluates the URL of the page a user is on, and looks for the appropriate templates in an order that goes from most specific to most broad. We already mentioned that every theme must have the most basic files: `header.php`, `index.php`, `sidebar.php`, `comments.php`, and `footer.php`. These are the basics (and the backups) that will be used if no other template files exist. However, a theme can have many more template files that may be used.

If you are on the homepage, WordPress will use either `home.php` or, if no `home.php` file exists, `index.php`.

If you are looking at an individual post, WordPress will use either `single.php` or, if no `single.php` file exists, `index.php`.

If you are looking at a WordPress page, WordPress will first use the page template that has been assigned, if none, then `page.php` or, if no `page.php` file exists, `index.php`. Page templates allow for unique styling of a given page.

If you are looking at a category archive (all of the posts in a given category—the display that happens when you click on a category), WordPress will first use the most specific category template: `category-slug.php` (the slug is typically the category name—slug templates were added in WP 2.9) or `category-id.php` (where `id` is the ID number of your category). If neither of these exist, then `category.php` is used. If no `category.php`, `archive.php` will be used. Otherwise, `index.php` is used. This format allows you to have different templates for each category.

There's more...

For more information, see: `http://codex.wordpress.org/Template_Hierarchy` and: `http://codex.wordpress.org/The_Loop_in_Action`

Template tags

Finally, we arrive at the concept of template tags. These are bits of code, specific to WordPress, that insert information from your MySQL database.

Getting ready

Each tag has a default action. This action can be extended or modified with parameters. You don't need to know PHP to use template tags. In fact, template tags make it easy for people who are not PHP programmers to use the dynamic nature and functionality of PHP.

How to do it...

Let's break things down. Here's a common example: you want to display a list of your categories. Guess what? A template tag will dynamically spit out the list. Saving your time—since you do not need to type them out individually. You can also add categories or rename an existing category, and these changes will automatically be available throughout the live site. Pretty neat? Here is how it works:

```
<?php wp_list_categories(); ?>
```

1. Template tags need to be wrapped in PHP tags, so they must start with `<?php` and end with `?>`. That's as much PHP as you need to know to access the basics. The next part is the tag itself: `wp_list_categories`.

2. Then, the parenthesis, and (like CSS) we need to include the semi-colon for syntax: `();`

3. If the parentheses are empty, the default settings will be used. However, you can optionally pass parameters to the tag within the parenthesis to modify the function. If you do this, the parameters must be enclosed in single quotes (`'parameter'`).

Of course, until you spend a lot of time in WP, you won't know what these parameters are. Luckily, a quick search in the codex will tell you all you need to know.

How it works...

For `wp_list_categories`, there are twenty parameters available. Let's take a look at an advanced example:

```
<?php wp_list_categories('title_li=&exclude=1,2&orderby=count&show_count=1'); ?>
```

`title_li=` is a tricky, but useful, starting point. The default settings for `wp_list_categories` sticks the word "Categories" above the list. If you want to put your own title, you put the value in like this: `title_li=' . __('My Own Title') . '` You can include HTML tags, so to wrap your title in a `<h2>` tag, it would look like this: `title_li=<h2>' . __('My Own Title') . '</h2>`

To display no title at all, the value is set to nothing (null): `title_li=`

The ampersand (&) allows us to use multiple parameters. It has nothing to do with the title.

exclude does exactly what you might think, it excludes specific category IDs from the list. The default action is to display all categories. To exclude more than one category, separate the IDs with a comma (no space).

orderby determines the order in which the categories are displayed. The default value is to order alphabetically, by name. Other values include: ID, slug, count, and term_group. Here, we order by the count which will display categories with the most posts first and those with the least number of posts last.

show_count is a Boolean operator. That means it is either false or true, accepting only one of two values (either 0 or 1). This parameter will include the total number of posts (in parenthesis) next to the category name. The default is 0 (false). In our example, we set the value to 1 (true).

There's more...

For more information, see: http://codex.wordpress.org/Stepping_Into_Template_Tags

The complete list of template tags can be found here: http://codex.wordpress.org/Template_Tags

Customizing Kubrik

Now that we are familiar with the pieces that control the look and content of your theme, let's apply this knowledge and make some changes to the default Kubrik theme.

Getting ready

The first step is to make a list of the changes that you want to make. Here's what we've come up with:

- Increase width to 980px
- Increase font sizes in sidebar
- Use a graphic header

We've picked 980px as our target width because this size is optimized for a 1024 screen resolution and works well in a grid layout. Several CSS adjustments will be necessary to realize this modification, as well as using an image editing program (we will be using Photoshop).

How to do it...

To increase the page width, the first step is to determine which entries in the CSS stylesheet are controlling the width. Using Firebug to inspect the page (as seen below), we find that the selector #page has a value of 760px for the width property. And #header has a width of 758px (less because there is a 1px left margin). The .narrowcolumn selector gives the main content column a width of 450px. And #sidebar has a width of 190px. Finally, #footer has a width of 760px.

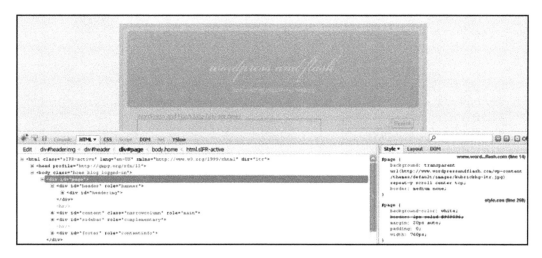

So, we will increase #page and #footer to 980px. #header we will increase to 978px. Let's apply all of the additional 220px width to .narrowcolumn. Taking note of the existing 45px left margin, our new value for the width property will be 700px. That means #sidebar width will remain at 190px, but the margin-left will need to be increased from 545px to 765px.

1. Click on **Appearance | Editor**.

2. In the right-hand column, below the **Templates** heading, click on **style.css**.

Scroll past the section that says **/* Begin Typography & Colors */**, until you get to the section that says **/* Begin Structure */**:

Make the following changes to the stylesheet (style.css), commenting as appropriate to document your changes.

```
#page {
    background-color: white;
    margin: 20px auto;
```

```
    padding: 0;
    width: 980px; /* increased from 760px */
    border: 1px solid #959596;
    }

#header {
    background-color: #73a0c5;
    margin: 0 0 0 1px;
    padding: 0;
    height: 200px;
    width: 978px; /* increased from 758px */
    }

.narrowcolumn {
    float: left;
    padding: 0 0 20px 45px;
    margin: 0px 0 0;
    width: 700px; /* increased from 450px */
    }

#sidebar {
margin-left:765px; /* increaseed from  545px */
padding:20px 0 10px;
width:190px;
}

#footer {
    padding: 0;
    margin: 0 auto;
    width: 980px; /* increased from 760px */
    clear: both;
    }
```

Adjustments via Photoshop

We'll also need to use an image editing program to modify the three background images that create the rounded corners: kubrikbg-ltr.jpg, kubrickheader.jpg, and kubrickfooter.jpg. In this example, we modify kubrik-ltr.jpg (the background image for #page), a 760px image.

1. Open up the image in Photoshop, select all, copy, create a new document (with a white or transparent background), and paste (*Ctrl-A, Ctrl-C, Ctrl-N, Ctrl-V*).

2. Increase the canvas size (**Image | Canvas Size**) to 980px, keeping the image centered on the left-hand side by clicking on the left-pointing arrow.

3. Select one half of the image with the Rectangular Marquee Tool, cut and paste.

4. Use the Move Tool to drag the new layer to the right-hand side of the canvas. In this case, it does not matter if you can see the transparent background or if your selection was exactly one half the image. Since the middle of the image is simply a white background, we are really only concerned with the borders on the left and right. The following screenshot shows the background image cut in half and moved over:

5. Save for Web and Devices, exporting as a jpg. Then, replace the existing `kubrikbg-ltr.jpg` with your modified version via FTP.

The steps are similar for both `kubrickheader.jpg` and `kubrickfooter.jpg`—. Increase the canvas size and copy/paste from the existing image to increase the image size without stretching or distortion. The only difference is that you need to copy and paste different parts of the image in order to preserve the background gradient and/or top and bottom borders.

In order to complete our theme customization, the width of `.widecolumn` will need to be increased from 450px to 700px (and the 150px margin should be converted to a 45px margin, the same as `.narrowcolumn`). Also, the `kubrikwide.jpg` background image will need to be modified with an image editing program to increase the size from 760px to 980px. Then, the individual post view will look as good as the homepage. By following the same steps as above, you should now be prepared to make this final customization yourself.

Our next goal is to increase the sizes of the sidebar fonts. Firebug helps us to pinpoint the relevant CSS. `#sidebar h2` has a font-size of 1.2em (around line 123 of `style.css`). Let's change this to 1.75em. `#sidebar` has font-size of 1em. Let's increase this to 1.25em.

To use a graphic in the header, open up `kubrickheader.jpg` in a new Photoshop document. Use the magic wand tool to select and delete the blue gradient with rounded corners. Now, use the rounded rectangle tool to insert your own custom header area. You can apply another gradient, if desired. We choose to apply a bevel and emboss texture to our grey rectangle. Then, to paste in some photos, decreasing their opacity to 50%.

In a short time, we've been able to modify Kubrik by re-writing CSS and using an image-editing program. This is the most basic technique for theme modification. Here is the result:

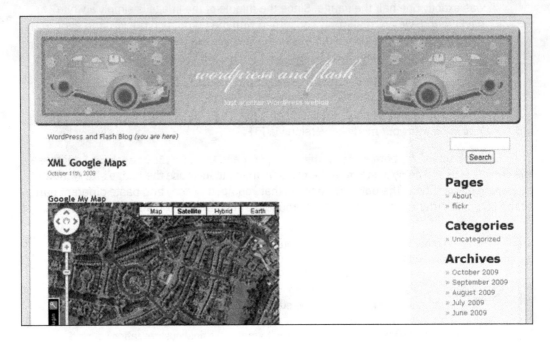

There's more...

Let's explore theme customization in more detail, continuing to use the default Kubrik theme. In the subsequent sections, we will add a second widgetized sidebar and create a custom template for a page. These final two goals provide the opportunity to apply our understanding of template hierarchy and the use of template tags.

Adding a widgetized sidebar

Adding a widgetized sidebar is an intermediate task. Let's make a unique sidebar which we can use in a custom page template.

First, let's add the CSS we'll need to the stylesheet. Our new sidebar is similar to the original. The larger font size and dashed border are the only stylistic differences:

```
#sidebar-custom {
padding: 0px 0 10px 10px;
width:190px;
margin-left: 765px;
border-left: 2px dashed #000000;
font-size: 1.5em;
}
```

We will also add our new selector to other stylesheet entries to avail ourselves of existing formatting:

```css
#sidebar h2, #sidebar-custom h2 {
    margin: 5px 0 0;
    padding: 0;
    }

#sidebar ul li, #sidebar-custom ul li {
    list-style-type: none;
    list-style-image: none;
    margin-bottom: 15px;
    }

#sidebar ul ul, #sidebar ul ol, #sidebar-custom ul ul {
    margin: 5px 0 0 10px;
    }
```

Now, let's create a the sidebar itself. Create a new document in your text editor. We start with a `<div>` to hold the contents of the sidebar. Then, start an unordered list, followed by a function to display whatever widgets have been enabled for the custom sidebar. Next, some data to display in case no widgets are being used. Then, the end of the unordered list and the end of the if statement, followed by the end of the custom sidebar. Save this document as `sidebar-custom.php` and upload to the theme directory:

```php
<div id="sidebar-custom">
<ul>
    <?php if ( !function_exists('dynamic_sidebar') || !dynamic_
sidebar('custom') ) : ?>
        <li><h2>Archives</h2>
            <ul>
            <?php wp_get_archives('type=monthly'); ?>
            </ul>
        </li>

        <?php wp_list_categories('show_count=1&title_
li=<h2>Categories</h2>'); ?>

        <?php wp_list_bookmarks(); ?>
    </ul>
        <?php endif; ?>
        </div> <!-- end sidebar-custom -->
```

The final step is to modify the theme functions to register our new sidebar. The easiest way to add multiple sidebars is like this:

```
register_sidebars(2);
```

Click on **Appearance | Editor** and click on `functions.php`.

You will see that Kubrik is set up to register a single sidebar:

```php
if ( function_exists('register_sidebar') ) {
    register_sidebar(array(
        'before_widget' => '<li id="%1$s" class="widget %2$s">',
        'after_widget' => '</li>',
        'before_title' => '<h2 class="widgettitle">',
        'after_title' => '</h2>',
    ));
}
```

Let's modify this entry to give the original sidebar a name (original), and then copy and paste the register sidebar function and give the second array another name (custom):

```php
if ( function_exists('register_sidebar') ) {
    register_sidebar(array(
        'name' => 'original',
        'before_widget' => '<li id="%1$s" class="widget %2$s">',
        'after_widget' => '</li>',
        'before_title' => '<h2 class="widgettitle">',
        'after_title' => '</h2>',
    ));

    if ( function_exists('register_sidebar') )
     register_sidebar(array(
       'name' => 'custom',
        'before_widget' => '<li id="%1$s" class="widget %2$s">',
        'after_widget' => '</li>',
        'before_title' => '<h2 class="widgettitle">',
        'after_title' => '</h2>',
    ));
}
```

For more information, see: `http://codex.wordpress.org/Widgets_API`

Creating a custom page template

It's easy to create a custom page template.

Start by creating some CSS for the new page. We'll use the `.narrowcolumn` entry as a starting point:

```
.customcolumn {
    float:left;
    padding:0   40px ;
    margin-left: 20px;
    width:665px;
    background: #F5B82A;
}
```

Now, create a new document in your text editor. The first thing you need is to declare the template name. This is wrapped in a PHP tag and commented out, as follows:

```
<?php
/*
Template Name: My Custom Page Template
*/
?>
```

Next, copy and paste the code that we will be starting with. In our case, we'll copy and paste the entire text of the `page.php` file from the default theme folder. You could use any existing template, such as `index.php` or `archive.php`, depending on your goals.

We also have the opportunity to use any template tags we choose in our page template. As an example, here we include the comment form:

```
<?php comments_template(); ?>
```

To use our new sidebar, simply modify the existing template tag:

```
<?php get_sidebar('custom'); ?>
```

To apply the new template, edit any page. In the **Attributes** menu on the right-hand side, there is a **Template** menu. Pull down to find and click to select the new template: **My Custom Page Template**. Click **Update Page** to save your changes. You can also apply a template via the **Quick Edit** menu in the **Edit Pages** screen:

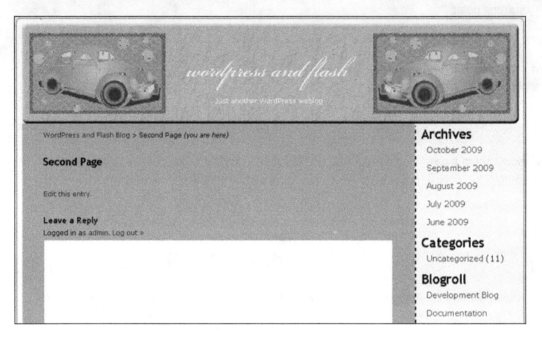

Here is the finished code:

```php
<?php
/*
Template Name: My Custom Page Template
*/
?>

<?php
/**
 * @package WordPress
 * @subpackage Default_Theme

 */

get_header(); ?>

    <div id="content" class="customcolumn" role="main">
<br /><div class="breadcrumb">
```

```
<?php

if(function_exists('bcn_display'))

{

    bcn_display();

}

?>

</div>
        <?php if (have_posts()) : while (have_posts()) : the_post(); ?>

        <div class="post" id="post-<?php the_ID(); ?>">

        <h2><?php the_title(); ?></h2>

            <div class="entry">

                <?php the_content('<p class="serif">Read the rest of this
page &raquo;</p>'); ?>

                <?php wp_link_pages(array('before' => '<p><strong>Pages:</
strong> ', 'after' => '</p>', 'next_or_number' => 'number')); ?>

            </div>

        </div>

        <?php endwhile; endif; ?>

    <?php edit_post_link('Edit this entry.', '<p>', '</p>'); ?>

    <?php comments_template(); ?>

</div>

<?php get_sidebar('custom'); ?>

<?php get_footer(); ?>
```

You have now learned the basics of theme customization. To summarize, many changes are made simply by modifying CSS rules. Other changes require the use of an image editing program. You've also learned how to add a widgetized sidebar, and how to create a custom page template that uses template tags to output content from the database. Keep studying, and practicing, and you will soon be able to modify any theme, or even create your own!

8
Flash Animations

In this chapter, we will cover the following:

- ▸ Creating a shape tween
- ▸ Creating a classic tween
- ▸ Creating a motion tween
- ▸ Using the Motion Editor
- ▸ Using motion presets
- ▸ Animating with the Bone tool
- ▸ Animating inside movie clips
- ▸ Creating a button

Introduction

This chapter covers creating your own Flash animations for your blog. The focus here is on animating in the Flash timeline. The lessons here are to help you with the fundamentals of Flash animation and give you a jump start on the process.

Using symbols is an important part of animating in Flash. There are three different types of symbols: graphic symbols, buttons, and movie clips. All symbols in Flash have some sort of timeline:

- ▸ The timeline of a graphic symbol allows multiple layers to exist in the same symbol, but not animation. Graphic symbols hold static information.
- ▸ A button has a timeline that is not time-based, but user-based. This means that the button symbol instance changes based on what the user does with their mouse, rather than on time passing. A button symbol can hold graphic symbol instances and movie clip symbol instances as well as multiple layers.

▸ A movie clip symbol has a robust timeline that accommodates multiple layers as well as animations that happen over time. Additionally, a movie clip symbol can hold graphic symbol instances, instances of different movie clips, and button symbol instances.

▸ Placing or creating something inside of a symbol is referred to as nesting.

Creating a shape tween

Shape tweens are used when you want to change one shape into a different shape. This is best done on a one to one ratio, for example, to change one circle into one star. Also, simple shapes will give you results that are at least somewhat predictable. Using a shape tween on complex shapes will often yield surprising results. If you try to use a shape tween to make it look like a caterpillar is morphing into a butterfly, you will get a tangled mess in the middle.

Shape tweens work on objects, primitive objects, and merged shapes.

How to do it...

1. In Flash, create a new file by going to **File | New** (*Ctrl/Cmd N*). Select Flash **File (ActionScript 3.0)** and hit **OK**.

2. *Double-click* on **Layer 1** and rename it **Shape Tween**.

3. Use any one of the drawing tools to create a shape or object of any size and color you want. Remember to keep it simple. For instance, create an oval by dragging the Oval tool on the stage.

4. *Right-click/Ctrl-click* on the key frame in the timeline and choose **Create Shape Tween**.

5. Select a frame several frames down the timeline (frame 10 or higher) and make a new key frame (*F6*). Change the color of the shape on this key frame.
Your timeline should look, roughly, like this:

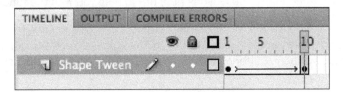

6. Hit *Return* to see the movie play inside of Flash. This is a basic shape tween.

7. Select the shape in the last key frame of your tween. Then, delete it. Make a different shape with a different tool. Make it whatever size and color you want. Place it where ever you want on the stage.

8. Hit *Return* to see the movie play in Flash. This is a morph effect.

9. Save the `FLA` file and test the movie (*Ctrl/Cmd Return*) to generate the `SWF` file.

How it works...

Shapes and objects in Flash are vector-based. Vectors have anchor points that describe the points where the line defining the edge of the shape or object changes direction. If the beginning and end shape have the same number of anchor points (especially in the same locations), the tween will work well and be visually predictable.

In a shape tween, Flash is trying to find the tween of least resistance. It is trying to make the mathematical change from one shape to another in the amount of frames you allotted by using the least amount of file size. It is also matching up the anchor points of your shapes as well as possible.

See also

▶ Creating a classic tween

▶ Creating a motion tween

Creating a classic tween

Classic tweens are used when you want to animate one symbol instance. The animation can be a transformation, such as rotation or scale, or a movement change. Also, with the use of symbol instances, color effects can be tweened so that a gradual color shift is possible.

 In previous versions of Flash (CS3 and prior), a classic tween is referred to as a motion tween.

Classic tweens are best used on symbol instances. Graphic symbols, movie clips, and buttons can have a classic tween applied to them. Any vector or bitmap can be converted into a symbol.

How to do it...

1. In Flash, create a new file by going to **File | New** (*Ctrl/Cmd N*). Select Flash **File (ActionScript 3.0)** and hit **OK**.

2. *Double-click* on **Layer 1** and rename it **Classic Tween**.

3. Use any one of the drawing tools to create a shape or object of any size and color you want. Alternatively, you can import (*Ctrl/Cmd R*) a file, such as a `JPG`, to use.

4. Select the item(s) that you want to animate. Go to **Modify | Convert to Symbol** (*F8*). For **Type**, choose **Graphic** to keep this simple. For **Name**, name the symbol **g_whateverItIs** (for example, if it's a circle, name it **g_circle**, if it's a red dog, name it **g_redDog**.). Hit **OK**.

5. *Right-click/Ctrl-click* on the key frame in the timeline that is holding the symbol instance and choose **Create Classic Tween**.

6. Select a frame several frames down the timeline (frame 10 or 20 or higher) and make a new key frame (*F6*). Your timeline should look, roughly, like this:

7. Use the Selection tool to move the symbol instance to a different location on the stage. For instance, if the symbol instance is on the left side of the stage at frame 1, move the symbol to the right side of the stage at your last frame so that the animation will show the symbol instance moving from left to right.

8. Hit *Return* to see the movie play inside Flash. This is a basic classic tween.

More key frames can be added to any animation when you want a change to happen in the animation. Select a frame and press *F6* to add another key frame. Change something about the symbol instance (such as its location). Changing the position of an element that is animated changes its direction.

9. Save the FLA file and test the movie (*Ctrl/Cmd Return*) to generate the SWF file.

How it works...

Classic tweens are used to animate one element changing over time. Flash moves the same symbol instance from one location or orientation to another over the course of the number of frames you specify. Every time you want a change in the animation (for example, rotation, direction, or scale), you must create a key frame. The key frames are the points in time where the symbol instance is drawn. The tweened, or transitional, frames are created through the automatic interpolation of the contents of the key frames. Basically, math is used to automatically render the tween so that you don't need to draw every single frame of the animation in Flash. This not only cuts down on the time you spend animating, it also reduces your file size.

There's more...

You can do a lot more:

Tweening color and Alpha changes

1. Select one of the key frames in your timeline by clicking on it.

2. Now, click on the symbol instance that is drawn on that key frame by clicking on it in the document window with the Selection tool.

3. In the **Properties** panel, change the **Style** from **None** to **Tint**:

4. Choose a tint color by either adjusting the sliders or clicking in the color rectangle to access a swatch panel. Also, choose a tint percentage. 100% will make the chosen tint color completely opaque over the top of your entire symbol instance.

5. If you prefer to change the transparency of the symbol instance, select **Alpha** instead of **Tint** from the **Style** drop down. Adjust the slider as desired:

   ❑ 0% makes the symbol instance completely transparent at the key frame selected.

   ❑ 100% makes the symbol instance completely opaque at the key frame selected.

6. Hit *Return* to see the movie play in the timeline in Flash.

See also

▶ Creating a shape tween

▶ Creating a motion tween

Creating a motion tween

Motion tweens as they currently exist is in Flash CS4 are new to Flash. In previous versions of Flash, the term motion tween was used. However, it was used to describe what is currently called a classic tween.

The process for setting up a motion tween is basically the same as that for setting up a classic tween. The difference is how they function after they are set up. It is very easy to make a motion tween follow a curved path rather than a straight line path. Also, motion tweens can be affected in a more advanced fashion through the use of the Motion Editor. Motion Presets also exist now that apply pre-made motion tweens to your selected symbol instance.

Like classic tweens, motion tweens can be applied to any symbol instance.

How to do it...

1. In Flash, create a new file by going to **File | New** (*Ctrl/Cmd N*). Select Flash **File (ActionScript 3.0)** and hit **OK**.

2. *Double-click* on **Layer 1** and rename it **Motion Tween**.

3. Use any one of the drawing tools to create a shape or object of any size and color you want. Alternatively, you can import (*Ctrl/Cmd R*) a file, such as a JPG, to use.

4. Select the item(s) that you want to animate. Go to **Modify | Convert to Symbol** (*F8*). For **Type**, choose **Graphic** to keep this simple. For **Name**, name the symbol **g_whateverItIs** (i.e.—if it's a circle, name it **g_circle**, if it's a red dog, name it **g_redDog.**). Hit **OK**.

5. *Right-click/Ctrl-click* on the key frame in the timeline that is holding the symbol instance and choose **Create Motion Tween**.

6. If your layer only had the initial key frame in it, Flash will provide one second's worth of frames for you. If your layer had more than the initial key frame in it, Flash will convert the existing frames into tweened frames but not generate additional frames. Your timeline should look, roughly, like this:

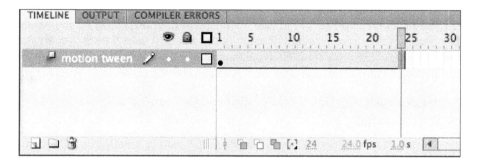

7. To add more time to your tween, select any frame and hit *F5* to simply add time, but leave the symbol instance unchanged. Hit *F6* to add a key frame so that you can change something about the symbol instance.

8. At any point in time in the timeline, move the playback head to a frame and hit *F6* to generate a key frame and adjust the symbol instance. You can use the Free Transform tool to rotate, skew, and change scale.

9. Notice that if you change the location of the symbol instance, a path that has dots on it appears that connects the symbol instances from location to location. Use the Selection tool to bend this path. Your symbol instance will now travel in a curved line.

How it works...

Motion tweens are object-based rather than timeline-based. This is different than how classic and shape tweens work. You are still able to set up the tween in much the same way. Adding basic key frames can also occur in the same way. The key frames show up as small diamonds instead of black circles since the symbol instance is not exactly redrawn at those points for a motion tween. The diamonds show the location of a change rather than a complete redraw.

See also

▸   Creating a shape tween
▸   Creating a classic tween

Using the Motion Editor

When you are using motion tweens to create your animation, you can use the Motion Editor to gain more control over the animation. The Motion Editor gives you the ability to change the location, scale, rotation, color effects, filters, and ease of your animation separately. You can address each of these properties in your animation at different points on your timeline without impacting other properties at that same point in time. It is as if each property has its own timeline inside of the motion tween. For instance, a symbol instance can change location without impacting a color effect change that was already taking place.

Getting ready

Use a file that already has a motion tween created. See *Creating a motion tween* if you need further instruction on accomplishing this. If you are new to Flash, start with a simple motion tween where the symbol instance only changes direction.

How to do it...

1. In your Flash file, select your tween span by clicking on the tweened frames in the timeline.

2. Go to **Window | Motion Editor** if the panel is not already accessible. It should look something like this for a basic animation:

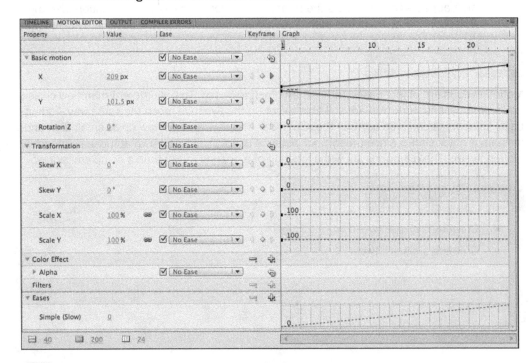

3. There are separate sections for **Basic Motion, Transformation**, etc. To the right, each section has settings that can be adjusted. At the far right, each editable property has a representation of the timeline illustrating how that property changes over time in the animation.

4. To adjust the position of the symbol instance at the start of the animation, move the playback head to the beginning of the timeline. Change the **x** or **y** coordinates by clicking on the blue numbers and typing in new numbers.

5. Test your movie (*Ctrl/Cmd Return*).

6. Back in the **Motion Editor**, also adjust the scale of your symbol instance. To make a change in scale part way through the animation, move the playback head into a position where there is not currently a key frame. Click on the diamond shape to the left of the timeline to add a key frame. Now, change the scale for that motion key frame.

7. If you wish to add a color effect, such as **Alpha** or **Tint**, click on the plus (**+**) button to the right of **Color Effect** and choose the desired effect. Select or create a key frame as needed. Change the settings available.

8. To add a filter, click the plus (**+**) button to the right of **Filters** and select a filter. Move the playback head over a key frame that already exists for **Filters** or create a new key frame. Change any settings.

9. **Ease** is a little more involved. The default ease setting is **Simple (Slow)**. You can make your animation ease in or out by adjusting the ease from -100 to 100. Negative numbers will ease your animation in. This means it starts slow and speeds up. Positive numbers ease your animation out so that it starts fast and then slows down. An ease of 0 keeps your animation at a constant rate all the way through it.

10. Add at least one more type of ease. To do this, click the plus (**+**) button to the right of Ease and choose one or more from the list. Some of the preset eases have specific uses in mind and are named to represent those uses (for example, Bounce is for making things bounce). You can also choose Custom and create your own ease with as many key frames as you need.

11. Now that you have more than one ease selected and/or edited, you can apply different eases to different elements. For instance, under **Basic Motion**, change the ease for **X** to **Simple (Slow)** and for **Y** to **Bounce**.

12. Test the movie (*Ctrl/Cmd Return*).

Any property listed/used in the Motion Editor can have an ease method applied to it. The ease applies to that property for the length of the entire tween span.

How it works...

The Motion Editor breaks your animation down into its separate editable parts and allows you to adjust them by creating individual-level key frames for those parts. A scale change can happen at a different point in time than a change in position. With a motion tween and the Motion Editor, those changes are kept track of and made editable in a more advanced and ultimately more controllable fashion.

Using motion presets

Flash CS4 has a number of pre-made motion tweens ready for you to use. In this recipe, you will apply motion presets to symbol instances.

Getting ready

Have a file open that contains a movie clip symbol instance. If you do not have such a file, make a new file in Flash, create a shape or import a file, and then go to **Modify | Convert to Symbol**. Name the symbol, choose **movie clip** for **Type**, and hit **OK**. You are ready to roll.

How to do it...

1. Go to **Window | Motion Presets** to get the **Motion Presets** panel if it is not already open.
2. Double-click on the **Default Presets** folder to gain access to the presets.
3. Select your symbol instance by clicking on it with the Selection tool.
4. Click on a preset, such as **fly-in-blur-left** and click **Apply**.
5. Save and test your movie (*Ctrl/Cmd Return*).

How it works...

Motion presets are saved tweens. The settings used to create an animation can be saved and reapplied to any other symbol instance. The **Motion Presets** work best on movie clips, but can also be applied to graphic symbols and buttons with differing degrees of success.

There's more...

The following section takes this discussion further.

Creating your own motion preset

1. Create a movie clip symbol instance.

2. Right-click on the key frame containing it in the timeline and choose **Create Motion Tween**.

3. Move the playback head (the red rectangle) to the last frame of the tween and hit *F6* to create a new motion key frame.

4. Change something about the symbol instance. For example, to create a fade-out effect, click on the symbol instance on the stage with the Selection tool. Then, go to the Properties panel and change the **Style** of the **Color Effect** to **Alpha**. Turn the **Alpha** down to 0%. Make sure the **Alpha** is still set to 100% at the first key frame.

5. Click on the tween span in the timeline to select it.

6. In the **Motion Presets** panel, click on the Save selection as preset button on the bottom left of the panel. Name the preset. This adds the motion tween settings to the **Custom Presets** folder for you to use at your leisure on any symbol instance.

See also

▸ *Creating a motion tween*

▸ *Using motion presets*

Animating with the Bone tool

The Bone tool is used to create an armature to connect and animate separate symbol instances. It is a direct way of controlling elements that are supposed to be animated in a sort of chain reaction like the movement of limbs. This recipe gives you the run down on how to get started with the tool.

You start out by figuring out what is going to be the trunk of your armature and then connect the branches to it. The trunk is fairly stationary (like a tree trunk) and the branches, or limbs, move.

Getting ready

You can use the `bonetool.fla` file in the `Chapter 9` folder. If you are already comfortable with this sort of animation, or are an intermediate Flash user, create your own file. In order for the Bone tool to work, each piece to be animated should be a symbol instance. You can take a look at `bonetool_done.fla` to see an example of an animation done with the Bone tool.

How to do it...

1. Select each symbol instance in turn with the Transform tool and move the transform point (the circle inside the bounding box) to the position a joint would be in. The demo file, `bonetool.fla`, is already prepped. Feel free to adjust any of the transform points.

2. Use the Bone tool (it looks like a bone in the Tool box) to connect the symbol instance that will serve as the torso (trunk) to each of the limbs (branches). Drag from the torso of the balloon man to one of his shoulders:

He swims...

3. After connecting the torso to the shoulder, connect the shoulder to the elbow.

4. Repeat this until all of the limbs are attached. The order you do this in is not important. If it seems that you are getting the armature coming out from the torso instead of the shoulder, connect the other shoulder first. If problems persist, zoom in (*Ctrl/Cmd +*) so you can aim better.

5. Once the armature is created with the Bone tool, animate the armature. The demo is a looping animation.

6. Select frame 40 for every layer you have and hit *F5* to extend the timeline to that frame. For the **armature** layer (it renamed itself), hit *F6* at the last frame so that the animation will loop.

7. Move the playback head (the red rectangle) to a frame about in the middle of the armature tween.

8. Grab the Selection tool and drag the different connection points around. Also, drag the end of the arms and legs around. Where you drag changes the amount of control you have over different branches of your armature.

9. Make as many key frames as you need by hitting *F6* on different frames in the timeline.

10. Save and test the movie (*Ctrl/Cmd Return*).

Animating inside movie clips

Movie clips are versatile sorts of symbols. Part of their power is that they can contain animations and other symbol instances. Whenever you need to have a repeating action in your animation, you can use a movie to contain the repetitive element. This way, you only need to animate it once instead of multiple times. More advanced examples of this technique are used in walk cycles.

In this recipe, you will create a movie clip symbol that has an animation inside it. Then, you will place multiple instances of this symbol on your stage. For an example of movie clips in action, take a look at the `movieclip.fla` file in the `Chapter 9` folder. The demo file shows both a beginner-level use of a movie clip to create animated bubbles, as well as an advanced use of a movie clip to animate the balloon man swimming.

How to do it...

1. In Flash, create a new file by going to **File | New** (*Ctrl/Cmd N*). Select **Flash File (ActionScript 3.0)** and hit **OK**.

2. Save the file as `movie_clip.fla`.

3. *Double-click* on **Layer 1** and rename it **Movie Clip**.

4. Create a shape, such as a circle.

 Anything more complex is also fine. For instance, imported files can also be used.

5. Select the shape and go to **Modify | Convert to Symbol**. Name it **mc_movie**, or whatever name seems appropriate. For **Type**, choose **Movie Clip**. Hit **OK**. Your shape is now nested inside of the movie clip symbol.

6. *Double-click* on the symbol instance on the stage to isolate it and gain access to its timeline. You are going to do your animation inside of the movie clip. Remember that a movie clip has a timeline that can hold multiple layers as well as animations. Zoom in as necessary.

7. Once you double-click, the top left of the stage should show the bread crumbs for your location inside the movie, such as **Scene 1** and then **mc_movie** (or whatever you named your symbol instance). Make sure that the breadcrumbs list the name of your symbol instance as the last (farthest right) of the breadcrumbs. If it's not the last one on the right, click on the breadcrumb that is the name of your movie clip so that it becomes the last one on the right. Many things can be nested inside a movie clip, such as bitmap images, drawing objects, and other symbol instances. If you double-click on one of these, you will isolate it and will be working in its timeline. Keep an eye on the breadcrumbs! Make sure that the last breadcrumb listed is the correct one for your purposes.

8. *Right-click/Ctrl click* on the key frame in the layer. Choose **Create Shape Tween**.

9. Select frame 10 and hit *F6* to duplicate your first key frame. Change something about the shape such as its scale or location or both.

10. Click on **Scene 1** at the top left of the stage to see your main timeline again. It should still only have one key frame even though your movie clip has ten.

11. Test the movie (*Ctrl/Cmd Return*). The movie clip loops continuously through its ten frames as the main timeline loops continuously through its single frame.

12. If you want a gap in time before the animation loops, the easiest way to accomplish this is to add blank frames to the end of the movie clip's timeline. *Double-click* on the symbol instance again to re-enter the movie clip. Select frame 11 and *hit F7*. Select frame 20, for instance, and hit *F5* to extend the amount of time that nothing shows up.

13. Test the movie (*Ctrl/Cmd Return*).

14. Back in Flash, click on **Scene 1** to see the main timeline again. Populate frame 1 with more instances of the movie clip by dragging instances of **mc_movie** from the **Library** panel onto the stage in different locations.

15. Test the movie (*Ctrl/Cmd Return*). The power of the movie clip should be clearer now. You can reuse the movie clip in the same key frame. This is useful for achieving effects such as snow or rain falling, or stars blinking in the sky.

16. Back in Flash, make a new layer and name it **Delay**. You can make additional layers and place the movie clip at different points of time so that the movie clips are not perfectly synced. This adds believability to your animation. Select frame 7 and hit *F7* to make a new blank key frame. Drag multiple instances of the movie clip from the **Library** to the stage. Since the animation inside the movie clip is 10 frames long, the movie clips that show up on frame 7 will start before the first movie clips have finished.

17. Make as many additional layers and staggered key frames containing your movie clip as you think necessary.

18. Add frames to your main timeline so that the movie clips have enough time to play and so that the looping of the main timeline is not obvious. Select frame 80, for instance, for each layer and hit *F5* to extend the duration of the movie.

19. Test the movie (*Ctrl/Cmd Return*), and then save the Flash file.

There's more...

As stated above, it is possible to not only put animations inside movie clips, but also other symbol instances inside movie clips. This means you can put a movie clip that contains an animation inside of another movie clip and then animate that.

Animating movie clips that contain movie clips

1. Open the `bonetool_done.fla` file from the `Chapter 9` folder. Also, leave your current file open. You are going to copy and paste frames from one file into a movie clip in the other.

2. In the `bonetool_done.fla` file, use the Selection tool to select all of the parts of the balloon man that you want to copy. Then go to **Edit | Copy** (*Ctrl/Cmd C*).

3. Go into the `movie_clip.fla` file you were working on earlier in this recipe. If you don't have a file, use a file of your choosing, or just create a new Flash file.

4. At the bottom left of the **Library** panel, click on the **New Symbol** button:

5. Name the symbol **mc_swimming**. For **Type**, choose **Movie Clip**. Click **OK**.

6. You should now be looking at a blank white stage with a plus sign in the middle of it. The timeline should have just one layer with one empty key frame. Select the empty key frame and go to **Edit | Paste in Place** so that all of the separate pieces of the balloon man get lined up correctly. The animation of the armature is now inside your movie clip symbol. Make sure that all of the layers show up for the same amount of time. *F5* will add frames to a layer.

7. At the top left of the stage, click on **Scene 1** to see the main timeline again.

8. Click on the New layer button at the bottom left of the timeline to make a new layer. *Double-click* to rename it **swimming**.

9. Select the key frame for the swimming layer and drag **mc_swimming** onto the stage. Place it outside of the stage area (the white area) at the bottom. You are going to make the swimmer swim up.

10. *Right-click/Ctrl-click* on the key frame for the swimming layer and choose **Create Motion Tween**. **Create Classic Tween** will also work just fine if you prefer it.

11. Select frame 80 (the last frame of the movie thus far) and hit *F6* to make a new key frame there. At that frame, select the symbol instance of **mc_swimming** and move it off the top of the stage.

12. Test the movie (*Ctrl/Cmd Return*) to see the full effect. This is the same theory used to create walk cycles. You just happened to create a swim cycle instead.

13. Adjust the tween(s) as much or as little as you like.

14. Remember that movie clip symbols can hold any number of layers and animations. They can also contain ActionScript and other symbols.

See also

▶ *Creating classic tweens*

▶ *Creating motion tweens*

Creating a button

Buttons are useful user interface elements. Buttons are a form of a symbol. They allow the user to trigger events as simple as a visual rollover, or as complex as controlling slideshows, and more. In this lesson, you will learn how to set up a button so that it has up, over, down, and hit states. Buttons can be made using text, vectors, and imported bitmap files.

How to do it...

1. In Flash, create a new file by going to **File | New** (*Ctrl/Cmd N*). Select **Flash File (ActionScript 3.0)** and hit **OK**.

2. Save the file as button.fla.

3. *Double-click* on **Layer 1** and rename it **button**.

4. Grab the Type tool. Click on the stage and type **Click here**.

5. Select the text with the Selection tool and go to **Modify | Convert to Symbol**. Name it **b_click**, or whatever name seems appropriate. For **Type**, choose **Button**. Hit **OK**.

6. *Double-click* on the symbol instance on the stage to isolate it and gain access to its timeline. Zoom in as necessary.

7. Once you double-click, the top left of the stage should show the breadcrumbs for your location inside the movie, such as **Scene 1** and then **b_click** (or whatever you named your symbol instance). Make sure that the breadcrumbs list the name of your symbol instance as the last (farthest right) of the breadcrumbs. If it's not the last one on the right, click on it so that it becomes the last one on the right.

8. There should just be four frames if the button was made correctly. The frames are not time-based, but user-based. Therefore, they are named **Up, Over, Down,** and **Hit**, instead of numbered. The text you converted into a symbol is written onto the **Up** key frame.

9. Select the key frame for **Over** by clicking on the frame below where it says **Over** on the timeline. Hit *F6* to make a copy of the previous key frame. Use the **Properties** panel or the fill color chip in the Tool box to change the color of the text.

10. Select the key frame for **Down** by clicking on the frame below where it says **Down** on the timeline. Hit *F6* to make a copy of the previous key frame. Use the **Properties** panel or the fill color chip in the Tool box to change the color of the text.

11. Select the key frame for **Hit** by clicking on the frame below where it says **Hit** on the timeline. Hit *F6* to make a copy of the previous key frame. Use the Rectangle tool to create a rectangle that completely covers the text. Make sure that it has a fill color. It does not matter what color you use. No one will see it but you.

The hit state is the active area of the button. Whatever exists in color on the hit state is the part of the SWF file that is active as a button. Therefore, if you have text only as your hit state, the user must hit the lines of the text in order to activate the button. This is not user friendly. A rectangle that completely covers the text is user friendly. The user needs to roll over or click on the nice, big, easy-to-hit rectangle to activate the button.

12. Test the movie (*Ctrl/Cmd Return*). In the SWF file, roll your mouse over the button to see the **Over** state. Click and hold your mouse button down on the button to see the **Down** state. Move or keep your mouse away from the button to see the **Up** state. You will not see the **Hit** state. The shape you made on the **Hit** state delineates the active area of the button. Where ever that shape exists, the button states will function. It's like an image map or hot spot.

13. Save and close the file.

Button symbols can have any number of layers. They can also contain movie clips and graphic symbols in addition to vectors, text, and imported bitmap images. However, a button cannot contain another button.

WordPress Resources

Here is a collection of links that you may find useful as you continue learning about WordPress.

- ▸ `http://www.alistapart.com`

  Advanced web design resources: *"For people who make websites."*

  A List Apart Magazine explores the design, development, and meaning of web content, with a special focus on web standards, accessibility, and best practices.

- ▸ `http://codex.wordpress.org`

  The WordPress bible, from the creators of WordPress.

  The codex contains all of the support documentation for WordPress. It is the technical document explaining how every aspect of WordPress works. The site is maintained by the developers of WordPress and supplemented with information posted by users and website designers. If you are using WordPress, you should be sure to review the codex.

  `http://www.justintadlock.com`

  Justin Tadlock is the author or the Hybrid Framework for WordPress. He has also authored several plug-ins and contributes his substantial coding experience and ability in popular WP support forums. He has been using WordPress since 2005. See his *Tutorials* section to learn about how to use PHP in WordPress.

- ▸ `http://lorelle.wordpress.com`

  Lorelle VanFossen is a blog evangelist. Her site is geared towards a beginning to intermediate audience. She provides blogging tips, teaches you how to use WordPress, and writes plugin reviews.

▶ http://www.justintadlock.com

Justin Tadlock is the author or the Hybrid Framework for WordPress. He has also authored several plugins and contributes his substantial coding experience and ability in popular WP support forums. He has been using WordPress since 2005. See his Tutorials section to learn about how to use PHP in WordPress.

"Helping you learn more about blogging and WordPress every day with help, tips, advice, and techniques for blogging and using WordPress and WordPress.com."

▶ http://www.perishablepress.com

WordPress, design and security by Jeff Starr, with contributing authors.

"Perishable Press provides high-quality, in-depth articles on web design and development, graphic design, social media, blogging, software, and more. Learn how to use WordPress, PHP, SQL, HTAccess, JavaScript, (X)HTML, and CSS to create beautiful sites that are usable, accessible, and secure."

▶ http://www.smashingmagazine.com/tag/wordpress

Learn about WordPress, themes, coding, design, and more. If you are starting out as a WordPress or website developer, Smashing Magazine is an invaluable resource.

"Founded in September 2006, Smashing Magazine delivers useful and innovative information to Web designers and developers. Our aim is to inform our readers about the latest trends and techniques in Web development."

▶ http://www.wp-community.org

Archive of WordPress podcasts. If you like to learn by listening, be sure to check out WP-Community.org.

▶ http://www.wpbeginner.com

Site to help beginners learn about WordPress, by Syed Balkhi.

"WPBeginner is a site for New Wordpress Users. We will have tips, tools, and other advices for all Wordpress users. This can also be a place for new Wordpress users to interact in the comments and help each other out if necessary."

▶ http://www.wpcandy.com

WordPress themes, plugins, tutorials and tips, by Michael Castilla, Dan Philibin and others.

"WPCandy was created on October 1st, 2007, as a blog on everything about WordPress, from the latest themes and plugins to tutorials and tips. Already on it's 3rd redesign, WPCandy is one of the top sites about WordPress and is still kickin' ass."

Also see: WPCoder.com and WPInspiration.com.

- `http://www.wphacks.com`

  WordPress themes, plug-ins, and hacks, by Kyle Eslick.

  "WP Hacks was originally created on October 1, 2007 as Hack WordPress, as a place to discuss all things WordPress. In addition to featuring a large variety of WordPress themes and providing reviews of WordPress plug-ins, Hack WordPress was set up to cover the world surrounding WordPress, including the latest WordPress hacks, news, tips, tricks, and how-to's of the popular open source blogging software."

- `http://www.yoast.com`

  Tips on optimizing WordPress, search engine rankings, analytics and website performance.

  Joost de Valk is an SEO consultant and web developer who lives in the Netherlands.

  "Tweaking websites is what we do here at Yoast, from search engine rankings, to speed to user experience."

B

Flash Resources

There are a multitude of resources available to help you with Adobe Flash and Macromedia Flash. As you know, this book focused on Adobe Flash CS4 and ActionScript 3.0 as they are used and implemented in WordPress. Many of the resources listed below have information or tutorials about other versions of Flash and ActionScript 2.0, in addition to further CS4 resources that are not covered in the scope of this book. The list below is in no way comprehensive. It merely offers suggestions.

My learning process came from a number of different sources, some of which are listed below. Over the course of my years of teaching, I have also been a student. A fellow instructor, Abigail Rudner (`http://www.rudner.com`), was a great help to me when I first started learning Flash and using ActionScript 2.0. Many books exist that are specific to Flash and ActionScript. For books, I suggest hunkering down in a bookstore to look through the selection to find the book(s) that meet your needs for subject matter, proficiency level, and writing style. I hope you found this book helpful!

A reasonable resource for information, articles, and links to more of each on Adobe Flash:

- `http://www.actionscript.org/`
- `http://www.flashmagazine.com/`

Pre-made Flash components (for purchase):

- `http://www.ohmyflash.com`
- `http://www.flashsources.net`
- `http://www.activeden.net/`

Resources for furthering your coding prowess and more:

- `http://www.adobe.com/devnet/flash/`
- `http://www.republicofcode.com/tutorials/`
- `http://www.tutorialized.com/tutorials/Flash/1`
- `http://www.flashandmath.com/`

C
Shortcut Keys

Keyboard shortcuts are a great way to speed up your workflow and to work more ergonomically (with less mousing). It's worth learning the shortcuts for any program you regularly use. In this section, you will find WordPress and Flash keyboard shortcuts. We also point you to URLs to learn keyboard shortcuts for Windows, Macintosh, and Firefox.

WordPress has built in shortcuts for the Visual Editor, the HTML Editor, and for Comment Moderation.

Please note that keyboard shortcuts work differently depending on your operating system and browser. We suggest using Firefox for maximum compatibility. Most (but not all) of the following shortcuts are available in Internet Explorer.

If you are using Firefox, use *Alt* + *Shift* + key.

If you are using Internet Explorer, you may use *Alt* + key (*Shift* is never needed when using the HTML Editor, but sometimes needed in the Visual Editor).

If you are using a PC, use the *Ctrl* key.

If you are using a Mac, use the *Cmd* (Apple) key instead of the *Ctrl* key.

WordPress Visual Editor keyboard shortcuts

In the Visual Editor, you have two ways to style your content. The first way is to select a bit of text and press the keyboard shortcut to style your selection. The other way is to start the tag by doing the keystroke, then typing your content, then keystroke again to specify the end tag.

- ▸ Bold: *Ctrl/Cmd b*
- ▸ Italics: *Ctrl/Cmd i*

- Underline: *Ctrl/Cmd u*
- Undo: *Ctrl/Cmd z*
- Redo: *Ctrl/Cmd y*
- Heading 1: *Ctrl/Cmd 1*
- Heading 2: *Ctrl/Cmd 2*
- Heading 3: *Ctrl/Cmd 3*
- Line Break: *Shift Enter*
- Insert Image: *Alt/Option Shift m*
- Insert a Link: *Alt/Option Shift a*
- Insert the Read More tag: *Alt/Option Shift t*
- Align Left: *Alt/Option hift l*
- Align Center: *Alt/Option Shift c*
- Align Right: *Alt/Option Shift r*
- Blockquote: *Alt/Option Shift q*
- Strikethrough: *Alt/Option Shift d*
- Unordered List (ul): *Alt/Option Shift u*
- Ordered List (ol): *Alt/Option Shift o*
- Publish the Post: *Alt/Option Shift p*

WordPress HTML Editor keyboard shortcuts

In the HTML Editor, you will typically use two keystrokes to apply formatting (to insert the start and end tags). Below we note the keystrokes that are different in the HTML Editor. The keystrokes from the Visual Editor list above will work, except for some small differences.

- Bold: *Alt/Option Shift b*
- Italics: *Alt/Option Shift i*
- Code: *Alt/Option Shift c*
- List Item (li): *Alt/Option Shift l*
- Insert the Date and Time: *Alt/Option Shift s*
- No Heading shortcuts
- No align left, right or center

WordPress Comment Moderation keyboard shortcuts

To use keyboard shortcuts for comment moderation, first enable this option by visiting Users | Your Profile | Enable keyboard shortcuts for comment moderation.

Navigation:

- *j*: down
- *k*: up

Perform Actions:

- *a*: approve comment
- *s*: mark comment as spam
- *d*: delete comment
- *z*: undo
- *u*: unapprove comment
- *r*: inline reply to comment (Esc to cancel)
- *q*: "Quick Edit" for rapid inline editing

Bulk Actions:

- *Shift a*: approve comments
- *Shift s*: mark comments as spam
- *Shift d*: delete comments
- *Shift u*: unapprove comments
- *Shift t*: move comments to Trash
- *Shift z*: restore comments from Trash

From: `http://codex.wordpress.org/Keyboard_Shortcuts`

Flash keyboard shortcuts

- *Ctrl/Cmd N* - New Document
- *Ctrl/Cmd O* - Open
- *Ctrl/Cmd W* - Close
- *Ctrl/Cmd S* - Save

- ▶ *Ctrl/Cmd Shift S* - Save As
- ▶ *Ctrl/Cmd C* - Copy
- ▶ *Ctrl/Cmd X* - Cut
- ▶ *Ctrl/Cmd V* - Paste
- ▶ *F5* - Add Frames
- ▶ *F6* - Add Key Frame - this will duplicate the previous Key Frame or create a Key Frame out of the selected Frame
- ▶ *F7* - Add Blank Key Frame
- ▶ *Shift F5* - Remove Frames
- ▶ *Shift F6* - Remove a Key Frame
- ▶ *F8* - Convert to Symbol
- ▶ *Ctrl/Cmd F8* - New Symbol
- ▶ *F9/Option F9* - ActionScript Panel
- ▶ *Spacebar* - Hand Tool to scroll
- ▶ *Spacebar Ctrl/Cmd* - Zoom In Tool
- ▶ *Spacebar Ctrl Alt/Cmd Option* - Zoom Out Tool
- ▶ *Ctrl/Cmd +/-* - Zoom in/out from center
- ▶ *Ctrl/Cmd J* - Modify Document Properties (i.e.- fps, size, bg color)
- ▶ *Ctrl/Cmd Enter* - Test Movie
- ▶ *Ctrl Alt/Cmd Option Enter* - Test Scene
- ▶ *Enter* - Play movie in Flash from the Frame the Playhead is on to the end
- ▶ *.* - Ahead one Frame
- ▶ *,* - Back one Frame
- ▶ *Shift .* - Playhead back to last Frame
- ▶ *Shift ,* - Playhead back to first Frame
- ▶ *Ctrl Alt/Cmd Option B* - Enable Simple buttons

Windows keyboard shortcuts

▶ http://support.microsoft.com/kb/126449

Mac keyboard shortcuts

▶ http://support.apple.com/kb/HT1343

Firefox keyboard shortcuts

▶ http://support.mozilla.com/en-US/kb/Keyboard+shortcuts

D

Site Planning

Before you pick a theme or jump in and start editing one, we strongly encourage you to do some site planning. Similar to any endeavor, your website plan provides a starting point and needed structure. A plan establishes priorities and metrics, which are what will be emphasized and how success will be measured.

Goals	SEO Plan	Functionality	Aesthetics	Content	Pick a Theme	Extend WordPress
What are your goals?	Keyword, Competition, Audience	What must users be able to do?	How should the site look?	Outline your initial content.	Free or Premium?	Research plug-ins and third-party solutions

Goals

It may seem obvious, but take the time to write down your goals. Of course you want to be on the first page of Google for your targeted keywords. That's why you'll be making an SEO plan. What else? If you are launching a new site, how many visitors do you hope to attract within the first six months and within the first year? If you are selling products or services, how many sales per month do you need to make? If you are launching a personal site, how many articles per week or month do you want to post? How many inbound links do you want to build in the first year? Be specific since this will help keep you on track as you develop, launch, and maintain your site.

SEO Planning

Since it is so easy to set up a WordPress site, knowing what distinguishes your site and what it is about is important. The basics of an SEO plan include: a 100 character site description (for your description meta tag—this is the text that will summarize your site when it comes up in search engines) and 15 keywords or phrases (for your keywords meta tag). This list of keywords will keep you on target as you develop on site SEO. These are the words that should be repeated throughout your site: as categories, in your title tags, alt tags, file names, and (most importantly) marked up as `<h1>`, `<h2>`, `<b>`, and `<a href>`, etc.

Your domain name is important in so many ways. It should be succinct, easy to remember, and not easily confused with another site. SEO is another consideration. Make sure that your most important keywords are in your domain name, if at all possible.

A site with good SEO clearly explains what your site is about, to both people and search engines. Don't forget to establish and research your targeted audience. Distinct user groups have varying levels of technical ability and different expectations and aesthetics. Establishing these parameters will help guide subsequent planning stages.

Look at your competition and establish your market niche. What is already being done? You can distinguish your site by offering something unique, or an improvement on what's already out there. What can you do better? This is your competitive advantage.

Do keyword research, using the Google AdWords keyword research tool, available here: `https://adwords.google.com/select/KeywordToolExternal`

Functional Requirements

What must visitors be able to do while on your site? Here are a few common examples: users should be able to comment, register, submit content, sign up for a newsletter, fill out a contact form, subscribe to an RSS feed, or make a purchase.

Many actions can be done using WordPress alone. Others will require plug-ins or other third-party solutions. You will need to research and evaluate how to accomplish each of your requirements with WordPress or existing plug-ins. For special projects, consider working with a WordPress consultant to custom code a solution for your specific needs.

Aesthetic Requirements

How should the site look? Each site has unique requirements: an online scientific or literary journal will have rather different constraints when compared to an e-commerce site or a user community.

It's always a good idea to keep your essential content "above the fold," or viewable without any vertical scrolling. Some sites keep all the content above the fold, though this is very different than the traditional blog format that lists many posts (or excerpts) on the homepage.

Additionally, take time to address each of the following design elements:

- Colors: Pick out colors and get the hexadecimal values. For a chart of colors, see: `http://www.morecrayons.com/`

- Image sourcing: Gather and prepare your images, resizing and saving your photos in `.jpg` format. If you need images, see the following stock photography website: `http://www.sxc.hu/`

- Fonts: What fonts will you use? Remember that users must have the font installed on their computer. For this reason, a best practice is to specify font families via CSS—a list of the fonts to be used, in the order specified, if available. Choose from the safe web fonts (which exist on all computers), specify fonts for Mac, Windows 95 to XP, or Vista. To use a non-standard web font, see Chapter 6: *WP sIFR Plug-in*. For help picking out your fonts, see: `http://www.typetester.org/`

- Graphic assets: In order to customize your theme, you will need to organize and prepare graphic assets such as a logo, header, backgrounds, buttons, ads, etc. These should typically be in `.gif` or `.png` format. Consider working with a graphic designer or a WordPress consultant, if necessary.

- Multimedia: Audio and video assets will almost always need to be resized, compressed, or exported to be optimized for the Web. Gather your source files and consider working with a Video editor, if needed.

Site Outline

Make an outline of all the content on your site. This includes your pages, categories, Tags and initial posts to launch, as well as sidebar, header, and footer content. You may also consider sketching out a content calendar which will include deadlines for adding new content after the site is launched.

Index

Symbols

.htaccess file 39
.swf
  embedding, in WordPress 12
  embedding in WordPress, steps 13, 14
  embedding in WordPress, working 15
  placing 10
µAudio plugin (version 0.6.2)
  activating 132, 133
  configuring 132
  downloading 132, 133
  installing 132, 133
  URL 132
  using 132

A

Abigail Rudner
  URL 231
absolute dimensions
  versus relative dimensions 20
Adobe Flash
  resources 231
  URLs 231
Adobe Media Encoder
  about 107
  edit export, settings 110, 111
  encoding, steps 108, 109
  encoding, working 109
  files, removing 112
  multiple files, encoding at once 112
AdWords Keyword Research Tool
  URL 40
A List Apart Magazine
  URL 227

ampersand (&) 198
Apache web server
  URL 16

B

Bone tool
  about 219
  using, steps 220, 221
Breadcrumb NavXT plugin (version 3.2.1)
  activating 44
  installing 44
  using 44
  working 45, 46
button
  creating, steps 225, 226
  editing 139
  sound effects, adding 140
  sound effects adding, steps 140-142
  sound effects adding, working 142
  using, in common library 137
  using in common library, steps 137, 138
  using in common library, working 139
button symbol 209

C

category archive view 10
classic tween
  about 211
  creating, steps 211, 212
  working 212
colors
  URL 241

common library
buttons, using 137
buttons using, steps 137, 138
buttons using, working 139
content
inputting, in HTML editor 35
inputting in HTML editor, steps 36
inputting, in Visual Editor 29
inputting in Visual Editor, steps 29
inputting in Visual Editor, working 30, 31
CSS
about 190
block elements 193, 194
comments 194
inline elements 193, 194
steps 190
working 191-193
CSS stylesheet 30
custom page template
creating 205-207

D

Datafeedr Random Ads V2 plugin (version 2.0)
about 184
activating 184
ads, adding to widgetized sidebar 185
Commission Junction, URL 184
downloading 184
flash animation adding, full embed code
used 185
homepage, URL 184
installing 184
Dean's FCKEditor 31
Digital Restrictions Management. *See* **DRM**
Digital Rights Management. *See* **DRM**
DRM 52
dynamic publishing
versus static publishing 21, 22

E

Elegant themes
URL 107
English language homepage
URL 177
exclude 198

Extensible Markup Language. *See* **XML**
external styles 30

F

Facebook Photos plugin
URL 56
Fast Stone Image Resizer
URL 99
FCKEditor
documentation, URL 34
for WordPress, URL 31
toolbar buttons, URL 34
URL 34
Featured Content Gallery plugin
activating 81
homepage, URL 81
installing 81
working 86
filters, Flash
adding 63
deleting 63
disabling 63
enabling 63
resetting 63
Firebug
edit and debug 11
URL 11
Firefox, keyboard shortcuts 237
Flash
effects, creating 60
effects creating, steps 60-63
filters, adding 63
filters, deleting 63
filters, disabling 63
filters, enabling 63
image gallery building in Flash in timeline,
steps 73-76
image gallery building in Flash in timeline,
working 77
image gallery building in Flash, timeline based
73
image gallery building with XML, steps 77-80
image gallery building with XML,
working 80, 81
image gallery building, XML used 77
movie clip, creating 60

slideshow building in timeline, steps 86-88
slideshow building in timeline, working 88
slideshow, building timeline based 86
slideshow building with XML, steps 90-93
slideshow building with XML, working 93
slideshow building, XML used 89, 90
symbols 209, 210
used, for creating watermarks 66
usedtext creating, type tool used 60

Flash animation
about 209
symbols, using 209, 210

Flash components 231

Flash detection
adding, with Flash-generated JavaScript 23
adding with Flash-generated JavaScript,
  steps 23-25
adding with Flash-generated JavaScript,
  working 25
adding, with SWFObject 2.x 16
adding with SWFObject 2.x, steps 17-19
adding with SWFObject 2.x, working 19

Flash document
Google Maps, integrating 179
Google Maps integrating, steps 180-182
Google Maps integrating, working 182, 183

Flash Feed Scroll Reader plugin. *See* **WP
  Flash Feed Scroll Reader plugin (version 1.1.0)**

Flash-generated JavaScript
used, for adding Flash detection 23
used for adding Flash detection, steps 23-25
used for adding Flash detection, working 25

Flash, keyboard shortcuts
. - (ahead one frame) 236
, - (back one frame) 236
about 236
Ctrl Alt/Cmd Option B (enable simple
  buttons) 236
Ctrl Alt/Cmd Option Enter (test scene) 236
Ctrl/Cmd C (copy) 236
Ctrl/Cmd Enter (test movie) 236
Ctrl/Cmd F8 (new symbol) 236
Ctrl/Cmd N (new document) 235
Ctrl/Cmd O (open) 235
Ctrl/Cmd Shift S (save as) 236
Ctrl/Cmd S (save) 235

Ctrl/Cmd V (paste) 236
Ctrl/Cmd W (close) 235
Ctrl/Cmd X (cut) 236
Enter (play movie in Flash from the Frame)
  236
F5 (add frames) 236
F6 (add key frame) 236
F7 (add blank key frame) 236
F8 (convert to symbol) 236
F9/Option F9 (ActionScript Panel) 236
Shift F5 (remove frames) 236
Shift F6 (remove key frame) 236
Shift , - (playhead back to frame 1) 236
Shift . - (playhead back to last frame) 236
spacebar Ctrl/Cmd Option - (zoom out tool)
  236
spacebar Ctrl/Cmd - (zoom in tool) 236
spacebar (hand tool to scroll) 236

Flash .swf files
embedding, in WordPress 12

Flash & WordPress
merging 8
merging, steps 9
merging, working 10
strategy, developing 8

Flexi Quote Rotator plugin (version 0.1.3)
about 163
downloading 163
homepage, URL 163
installing 163

Flickr Manager plugin
URL 56

Flickr photo album plugin
activating 53, 54
advantages 53
images, sharing 53
installing 53, 54

Flickr Tag plugin
URL 56

FLIR
URL 176

FLV Embed (version 1.2.1)
about 98, 99
activating 99
configuring 100
installing 99
URL 98

working 101, 102
fonts
   URL 241
Free WP Tube (version 1.0)
   about 105
   activating 106
   installing 105
   URL 105
FTP client 12

G

Google AdWords keyword research tool
   URL 240
Google Analytics
   activating 46
   adding, steps 46, 47
   installing 46
   URL 46
   using 46
   working 47
Google Maps
   Google Maps API for Flash library,
      downlaoding 180
   Google Maps API library, URL 179
   Information Bubble, adding 184
   integrating, into Flash document 179
   integrating into Flash document,
      steps 180-182
   integrating into Flash document, working
      182, 183
   types 183
   zoom levels 183
Google Maps API key
   URL 177
Google Maps API library
   URL 179
Google XML Sitemaps plugin
   activating 41
   installing 41
   using 41
   working 41
graphic assets
   URL 241
graphic symbol 209

H

Hana FLV Player
   URL 103
home page 10
HTML character codes
   URL 45
HTML editor
   content, inputting 35
   content inputting, steps 36

I

IDs
   finding 85
image
   borders, adding 64
   borders, exporting as jpg files 64-66
image gallery
   building in Flash in timeline, steps 73-76
   building in Flash in timeline, working 77
   building in Flash, timeline based 73
   building in Flash with XML, steps 77-80
   building in Flash with XML, working 80, 81
   building in Flash, XML used 77
image sourcing
   URL 241
inline styles 30
iTag
   URL 177

J

jEdit
   URL 12
jQuery
   URL 34
Justin Tadlock
   URL 227
JW FLV Media Player
   URL 98

K

keyboard shortcuts
   Firefox 237
   Flash 235
   Mac 237

Windows 237
WordPress Comment Moderation 235
WordPress HTML Editor 234
WordPress Visual Editor 233
Kimli flash embed plugin
  URL 13
  used, for embedding .swf 12
Kubrik
  adjustments, via photoshop 200, 201
  customizing, steps 199, 200
  custom page template, creating 205-207
  widgetized sidebar, adding 202-204

L

lightbox effects
  about 56
  used 57
Lorelle VanFossen
  URL 227

M

Mac, keyboard shortcuts 237
MLA standard 52
Motion Editor
  about 216
  creating, steps 216, 217
  working 218
motion presets
  about 218
  creating, steps 219
  using, steps 218
  working 218
motion tween
  about 214
  creating, steps 214, 215
  working 215
movie clips
  animating 221
  animating, steps 221-223
  animating, that contain movie clips 223, 224
movie clip symbol 210
MP3 player
  coding, steps 151-153
  coding, working 153
  designing 146
  designing, steps 146-150

designing, working 150
  song information, displaying 154, 155
multimedia
  URL 241
MySQL database
  backing up, WP-DBManager plugin used 48

N

NextGen gallery plugin
  activating 70
  configuring 71, 72
  images, adding 70
  images, uploading 71
  installing 70
  watermarking options 71
NotePad
  URL 12

O

orderby 198

P

Perishable Press
  URL 228
permalinks 39
PodPress plugin (version 8.8.1)
  activating 135-137
  downloading 135-137
  installing 135-137
  URL 134
  using 134
Pre-made Flash components 231
preset skins
  autoplay, stopping 117
  Fullscreen mode, setting up through
        Flash 118-121
  hiding 116
  showing 116
  types 113
  using 113
  using, steps 113-115
  working 115

Q

quicktags 36
  URL 36
Quote Rotator
  creating, steps 168-170
  text, fading 171
  working 170

R

relative dimensions
  versus absolute dimensions 20
resources, Adobe Flash
  URL 231
resources, flash components
  URL 232
resources, for coding
  URL 232

S

SEO plan 240
SEO strategy
  creating, steps 40
SEO Title Tags plugin (version 2.3.3)
  activating 43
  installing 43
  URL 42
  working 43
shape tween
  about 210
  creating, steps 210, 211
  working 211
show_count 198
simple On/Off music button
  coding 144
  coding, steps 144, 145
  coding, working 145, 146
site
  backing up 48
  backing up, steps 48
  backing up, working 49
site, planning
  aesthetic requirements 240, 241
  functional requirements 240

  goals 239
  outline 241
  SEO planning 240
skin
  customizing, steps 122, 123
  customizing, Video Component buttons
    used 122
  customizing, working 124
  Video Component buttons, modifying 124
slideshow
  building in Flash in timeline, steps 86-88
  building in Flash in timeline, working 88
  building in Flash, timeline based 86
  building in Flash with XML, steps 90-93
  building in Flash with XML, working 93
  building in Flash, XML used 89, 90
  loop, stopping 88, 89
  slides, swapping 89
  start button, adding 94
  showstop button, adding 94
slideshows
  adding 81
Smashing Magazine
  URL 228
sound effects
  adding, to button 140
  adding to button, steps 140-142
  adding to button, woking 142
  adding, to over state 142
  adding, to timeline 142
  adding to timeline, steps 143
  adding to timeline, working 143
SoundManager2
  URL 130
static publishing
  versus dynamic publishing 21, 22
SWFObject 2.x
  used, for adding Flash detection 16
  used for adding Flash detection, steps 17-19
  used for adding Flash detection, working 19
symbols, Flash
  button symbol 209
  graphic symbol 209
  movie clip symbol 210
  timeline 209
  types 209

T

Tagnetic Poetry plugin (version 1.0)
activating 161
downloading 161
Flash source files, accessing 162, 163
installing 161
source files, URL 162
tag cloud, inserting 162
template files
about 194
steps 195
working 196
template tags
about 196
steps 197
URL 198
working 197, 198
Text Editor 12
theme
about 10
selecting 189
selecting, tips 190
Theme editor
theme template files, editing 36
theme template files editing, steps 37, 38
theme template files editing, working 38
theme structure
about 194
steps 195
working 196
theme template files
editing, in theme editor 36
editing in theme editor, steps 37, 38
editing in theme editor, working 38
template, hierarchy 38
TinyMCE
about 34
URL 34
TinyMCE Advanced plugin 31
title_li= 197
Two CSS stylesheets
URL 187

U

u (unapprove comment) 235

V

Video Component buttons
customizing 124, 126
using, to customize skin 122
Visual Editor
content, inputting 29
content inputting, steps 29
content inputting, working 30, 31
extending, with plugins 31
extending with plugins, steps 31-34
extending with plugins, working 34
Visual Editor, keyboard shortcuts
Alt/Option Shift a (insert link) 234
Alt/Option Shift c (align center) 234
Alt/Option Shift d (strikethrough) 234
Alt/Option Shift l (align left) 234
Alt/Option Shift m (insert image) 234
Alt/Option Shift o (ordered list) 234
Alt/Option Shift p (publish post) 234
Alt/Option Shift q (blockquote) 234
Alt/Option Shift r (align right) 234
Alt/Option Shift t (insert read more tag) 234
Alt/Option Shift u (unordered list) 234
Ctrl/Cmd 1 (heading 1) 234
Ctrl/Cmd 2 (heading 2) 234
Ctrl/Cmd 3 (heading 3) 234
Ctrl/Cmd b (bold) 233
Ctrl/Cmd i (italics) 233
Ctrl/Cmd u (underline) 234
Ctrl/Cmd y (redo) 234
Ctrl/Cmd z (undo) 234
Shift Enter (line break) 234

W

watermarks
creating, Flash used 66
creating, steps 66-68
creating, working 68
multiple images 68
multiple images, exporting as jpg files 68-70

WebTV plugin (version 0.6)
about 103
activating 103
installing 103
widgetized sidebar
adding 202-204
Windows, keyboard shortcuts 237
WordPress
Breadcrumb NavXT plugin (Version 3.2.1),
    using 44
configuring 38
configuring, steps 39
configuring, working 39, 40
Datafeedr Random Ads V2 plugin (version 2.0)
    184
Featured Content Gallery plugin 81
Flash .swf files, embedding 12
Flash .swf files embedding, steps 13-15
Flash .swf files embedding, working 15
Flexi Quote Rotator plugin (version 0.1.3) 163
FLV Embed (version 1.2.1) 98
free themes, selecting 189
free themes selecting, tips 190
Free WP Tube (version 1.0) 105
Google Analytics, using 46
Google XML Sitemaps plugin, using 41
HTML editor, content inputting in 35
NextGen gallery plugin 70
PodPress plugin (version 8.8.1) 134-137
Quote Rotator creating, XML used 167-170
SEO Title Tags plugin (Version 2.3.3),
    using 42
site, backing up 48
Tagnetic Poetry plugin (version 1.0) 161
theme template files, editing in theme
    editor 36
Visual Editor, content inputting in 29
Visual Editor, extending with plugins 31
WebTV plugin (version 0.6) 103
WordPress Multibox plugin 57
WPAudio Player plugin
    (version 1.5.2) 130-132
WP-Cumulus plugin (version 1.22) 158
WP Flash Feed Scroll Reader plugin (version
    1.1.0) 186
WP sIFR plugin (version 0.6.8.1) 172
XML Google Maps plugin (version 1.12.1) 176

µAudio plugin (version 0.6.2) 132, 134
WordPress bible
URL 227
WordPress codex
URL 36, 159
WordPress Comment Moderation, keyboard
    shortcuts
a (approve comment) 235
d (delete comment) 235
j (down) 235
k (up) 235
q (235
r (inline reply to comment) 235
Shift a (approve comments) 235
Shift d (delete comments) 235
Shift s (mark comments as spam) 235
Shift t (move comments to Trash) 235
Shift u (unapprove comments) 235
Shift z (restore comments from Trash) 235
s (mark comment as spam) 235
u (unapprove comment) 235
z (undo) 235
WordPress & Flash
merging 8
merging, steps 9
merging, working 10
strategy, developing 8
WordPress HTML Editor, keyboard shortcuts
Alt/Option Shift b (bold) 234
Alt/Option Shift c (code) 234
Alt/Option Shift i (italics) 234
Alt/Option Shift l (list item) 234
Alt/Option Shift s (insert date and time) 234
WordPress Multibox plugin
about 57
activating 57
installing 57
working 59
WordPress themes 189
WPAudio
URL 130
WPAudio Player plugin (version 1.5.2)
activating 130, 131
downloading 130, 131
installing 130, 131
using 130

WPBeginner
  URL 228
WPCandy
  URL 228
WP-Cumulus plugin (version 1.22)
  about 158
  activating 158
  authors homepage, URL 159
  downloading 158
  homepage, URL 158
  installing 158
  source files, accessing 160, 161
  source files, URL 160
  working 159
WP-DBManager plugin
  MySQL database, backing up 48
**WP Flash Feed Scroll Reader plugin (version
    1.1.0)**
  about 186
  activating 186
  downloading 186
  homepage, URL 186
  installing 186
  Two CSS stylesheets, URL 187
WP forums
  URL 137
WP Hacks
  URL 229
WP-iPodCatter
  URL 134
wp_list_categories 197
WP sIFR plugin (version 0.6.8.1)
  about 172
  activating 172
  downloading 172
  FLIR, URL 176
  homepage, URL 172
  installing 172
  More Info Section 176
  online font converter link, URL 172
  sIFR version, selecting 173
  support documentation, URL 176
  URL 172
  verification word, entering 174
  working 176
WP template hierarchy
  URL 38

X

XHTML 35, 52
XML 52
XML Google Maps plugin (version 1.12.1)
  about 176
  downloading 177
  English language homepage, URL 177
  geo-tagged Flickr stream, inserting 178
  Google Maps API key, URL 177
  installing 177
  iTag, URL 177
  map, inserting 178

Z

zoom, Google Max
  levels 183
zoom in tool 236
zoom out tool 236

Thank you for buying
Wordpress and Flash 10x Cookbook

Packt Open Source Project Royalties

When we sell a book written on an Open Source project, we pay a royalty directly to that project. Therefore by purchasing Wordpress and Flash 10x Cookbook, Packt will have given some of the money received to the Wordpress project.

In the long term, we see ourselves and you—customers and readers of our books—as part of the Open Source ecosystem, providing sustainable revenue for the projects we publish on. Our aim at Packt is to establish publishing royalties as an essential part of the service and support a business model that sustains Open Source.

If you're working with an Open Source project that you would like us to publish on, and subsequently pay royalties to, please get in touch with us.

Writing for Packt

We welcome all inquiries from people who are interested in authoring. Book proposals should be sent to author@packtpub.com. If your book idea is still at an early stage and you would like to discuss it first before writing a formal book proposal, contact us; one of our commissioning editors will get in touch with you.

We're not just looking for published authors; if you have strong technical skills but no writing experience, our experienced editors can help you develop a writing career, or simply get some additional reward for your expertise.

About Packt Publishing

Packt, pronounced 'packed', published its first book "Mastering phpMyAdmin for Effective MySQL Management" in April 2004 and subsequently continued to specialize in publishing highly focused books on specific technologies and solutions.

Our books and publications share the experiences of your fellow IT professionals in adapting and customizing today's systems, applications, and frameworks. Our solution-based books give you the knowledge and power to customize the software and technologies you're using to get the job done. Packt books are more specific and less general than the IT books you have seen in the past. Our unique business model allows us to bring you more focused information, giving you more of what you need to know, and less of what you don't.

Packt is a modern, yet unique publishing company, which focuses on producing quality, cutting-edge books for communities of developers, administrators, and newbies alike. For more information, please visit our website: www.PacktPub.com.

WordPress Theme Design

ISBN: 978-1-847193-09-4 Paperback: 224 pages

A complete guide to creating professional WordPress themes

1. Take control of the look and feel of your WordPress site

2. Simple, clear tutorial to creating Unique and Beautiful themes

3. Expert guidance with practical step-by-step instructions for theme design

4. Design tips, tricks, and troubleshooting ideas

WordPress Complete

ISBN: 978-1-904811-89-3 Paperback: 304 pages

A comprehensive, step-by-step guide on how to set up, customize, and market your blog using WordPress

1. Clear practical coverage of all aspects of WordPress

2. Concise, clear, and easy to follow, rich with examples

3. In-depth coverage of installation, themes, syndication, and podcasting

Please check **www.PacktPub.com** for information on our titles